RELATIONSHIP ADVICE THAT ACTUALLY WORKS

Jacob Lucas

ISBN: 978-1-3999-7537-7

Cover design by: Jacob Lucas

CONTENTS

INTRODUCTION

Welcome to *'Relationship Advice That Actually Works'* by Professional Dating & Relationship Coach, Jacob Lucas.

Do you want to be happy in your relationship?

Do you want to be in a relationship where you and your partner treat each other the right way?

Do you want relationship advice that ACTUALLY WORKS?

If you answered 'YES' to these questions this is the book for you!

Like many others, you want to be in a loving, fulfilling, happy relationship. You want someone to share life experiences with, someone you love to come home to, someone to grow old with, someone you feel connected with in lots of different ways, and much more! However, sometimes you come across barriers that can stop you from having the amazing relationship that you deserve.

The advice in this book uses a combination of psychology, social dynamics, and real-life experiences to help you understand your relationship better and guide you to have a much happier love life.

Sometimes it can feel like the questions you have about your relationship are complicated, but once you have learnt how to approach different situations in your relationship the right way, you'll find that the answers on how to have a successful relationship can be very simple.

I have coached many wonderful people across the world in their relationships and helped them achieve the type of relationship they've always dreamed of, and I hope this book does the same for you.

It's my pleasure to share relationship advice with you that ACTUALLY WORKS!

Let's begin…

5 QUALITIES EVERY RELATIONSHIP NEEDS TO BE SUCCESSFUL

From all of the evidence I have seen in my time as a dating and relationship expert, there are 5 main qualities that a relationship needs to be successful.

I want you to view a relationship like a house. For it to be a strong house that will stand the test of time, it needs to be built upon good foundations. If a house is built upon shaky foundations, the house will collapse. It's exactly the same for relationships.

Now I want you to view each of the 5 qualities in this chapter as one of the pillars that holds up your relationship and keeps it strong. If one of these pillars collapses, then the whole relationship collapses too. All of these 5 qualities work in harmony and are needed to keep your relationship a happy and successful one.

When you read the more specific advice in this book, you'll realise that the advice will use at least one of these qualities as it's foundation for the advice to work. It's great to keep that in mind as you'll see why some areas of your relationship are successful and some aren't.

Here are the 5 qualities that every successful relationship needs...

Good Communication

For a relationship to work you need to be able to communicate effectively with each other.

How you communicate with your partner is one of the most important parts of a relationship. With good communication you can overcome many different obstacles in your relationship and form a stronger bond with your partner as time goes on. But if one of you has poor communication, the relationship is always going to be hard work, and most of the time the relationship will come to an end.

You need to learn each other's communication styles.

Many people differ in the way that they communicate, and it can be very frustrating when you don't understand each other. This is where you need to recognise that everyone is different. Some of us are a lot more similar than others, but we all have our little differences that make us unique.

This doesn't mean that it can't be a strong relationship though because you have different communication styles. It just means that sometimes you will have to be extra patient and learn how your partner communicates. For example, some people like to communicate their feelings through their words, whereas some people communicate by their actions. If they have good intentions, then that is all that matters.

If you and your partner have very different communication styles and it's causing a lot of issues in your relationship, have no fear. Within this book there is clear advice for you and your partner to follow to overcome many obstacles that you are facing in your relationship, regardless of whether you have different styles of communication.

You both have good morals

Morals are extremely important in a relationship. Having good shared morals is one of the most important elements to whether you and your partner will have a successful relationship or not.

At times you can have minor differences in your moral views. However, most of the time, for a relationship to be successful, both of your moral views need to be well aligned.

I conducted some research about what people look for in a partner, and one of the most common answers was 'good morals'.

I agree with this myself, as there is nothing more unattractive than somebody who has bad morals.

If you and your partner's moral views align very well, then most of the time you will have a healthy and successful relationship.

However, a relationship will always end if one partner has good moral values and the other has bad moral values.

For example, let's say one partner has good morals and is very loyal, whereas the other partner has bad morals and is not loyal and cheats on their partner... This relationship will never work. This will cause many arguments and it is abusive behaviour, and the person with good morals must end the relationship. There are many examples like this, but the result is always the same... The relationship will fail if there are conflicting moral values.

You must be attracted to your partner

No matter what anybody says to you, attraction in a relationship is an absolute necessity! If people think that you can have a loving, happy, healthy, long lasting sexual relationship with someone you don't find attractive, then they are living in a fantasy world.

You can really like someone and think they are an amazing person, but you must have a sexual connection with them to have the best relationship possible. You should look at your partner and think they are very attractive. If you don't, then they aren't the right person for you. It may sound harsh, but it's the truth.

I see many couples who don't find their partner attractive, and it creates a lot of problems. They will get bored of their partner, they may end up cheating, or they simply feel very unfulfilled in their relationship and end up leaving their partner.

Having a healthy sex life with your partner, who you find very attractive, is one of the most important elements of your relationship, because it's something that only you two share with each other, and that's something very special and NEEDED in a successful relationship.

The only time when having a good sex life with your partner isn't a necessity is when someone has a medical reason as to why they can't have sex, which is a perfectly good reason! A good partner will be very understanding of this and will be as patient as their partner needs them to be.

Something that I see very often is people 'settling' for someone they don't find attractive because they don't think they can do better. This all stems from a lack of confidence, social conditioning, and possibly many other factors. These types of relationships never work because the tension and unease they feel within themselves manifest in a different way and their frustrations may get projected onto their partner, and that's not fair on them.

So, it's simple... You got to find your partner attractive to have a 100% fulfilling relationship.

Every successful relationship has good teamwork

Teamwork makes the dream work! When you enter a relationship with someone you become a team. Many of the decisions that you make in your life will impact your partner's life too.

You want to have a partner who makes decisions based on what's best for the relationship. If you have a partner who doesn't understand the value of teamwork, then you will have an incredibly frustrating partner to be with.

Whether it's the small day to day decisions, handling money in the relationship, coming to compromises when you've had a disagreement, a good couple will come together and do what's best for the relationship and each other.

You both need to see each other as equals. If one of you sees the other as inferior, then it's going to be a very unhealthy relationship.

You will both have your strengths and your weaknesses. But as a team you understand this and know when to let one person take the lead and the other person to follow in different scenarios. Once you both understand how to use your strengths in an effect way, you can achieve incredible things together!

Throughout this book teamwork will be a massive factor in making your relationship a happy one. You can put in 100% effort to make your relationship work, but if your partner isn't matching that energy then the relationship is doomed to fail. BUT if you both put in 100% effort, then I have no doubt that you and your partner will be able to overcome most of the challenges that you encounter in your relationship.

You and your partner need to have aligned life goals

To make a relationship successful in the long term, you and your partner need to have many of your life goals aligned. It makes the relationship very tricky to navigate if you don't have similar life goals.

For example, if you want to have children one day but you partner doesn't, then that relationship won't work.

Another example could be if you want to focus on your career, but your partner wants to go and travel the world. This wouldn't work because one of you will be off exploring the world whilst the other is at home, so you're not spending any quality time together.

Also, with different life goals comes different mentalities. If you have a growth mindset and want to achieve great things in your life but your partner doesn't, then you won't have much to talk about, and the relationship will eventually come to an end anyway.

But if you have well aligned life goals then you can build a wonderful life together. You can make plans to achieve these life goals you share, you'll have a lot to talk about, and you will be able to grow together.

All the happy couples in healthy relationships that I have met have well aligned life goals.

So, think about you and your partner... Are your life goals aligned, or do you both want different things out of life?

ALPHA, BETA & SIGMA PERSONALITY TYPES IN RELATIONSHIPS

In this chapter I am going to explain the 3 different personality types and how they function in relationships with the other personality types. It's a very interesting topic and it will be good for yourself to see which personality type you and your partner identify with the most.

Once you understand these personality types a little more, it will help you navigate different areas of your relationship, and help you understand the dynamics between you and your partner much better.

First of all, these are the traits of an Alpha, Beta, and Sigma personality type...

The Alpha

These are the main traits of an Alpha personality type:

- Natural leader
- Dominant
- Extroverted
- Seeks the approval of others
- Egotistical
- Not a good team player unless they are in charge
- Decisive
- Very Social
- Protective of their loved ones
- Prideful
- Usually the most aggressive personality type
- Comfortable with conflict

The Beta

These are the main traits of a Beta personality type:

- Follows. Does not lead.
- Submissive
- Can be either extroverted or introverted, but usually introverted
- Seeks the approval of others
- Doesn't naturally have a big ego, but can develop one under certain circumstances
- Great team player
- Indecisive

- Social
- Likes to feel protected
- Friendly
- Avoids conflict

The Sigma

These are the main traits of the Sigma personality type:

- Lone wolf
- Excellent leader but doesn't actively seek leadership roles
- Introverted
- Very independent
- Doesn't seek the approval of others
- Isn't egotistical
- Doesn't put a big emphasis on socialising. (However, Female Sigma's are more social than Male Sigma's)
- Great team player but prefers to work alone
- Decisive
- Stoic
- Loyal
- Protective of their loved ones
- Avoids conflict but is comfortable with conflict if it is forced upon them
- VERY dismissive to those who disturb their peace

Which personality type do you identify with the most?

As you can see there are many differences between an Alpha, Beta and Sigma. Whenever these different personality types interact with each other it can be complex. However, usually, you can tell how a relationship will be by what personality types are in the relationship.

Now I'm going to match up these different personality

types and explain how they function in a relationship with each other and if they are a good match for each other or not...

Alpha & Alpha

When there are 2 Alphas in a relationship, it very rarely works. This is because there are too many big egos in this type of relationship, and it usually leads to many conflicts.

2 Alphas in a relationship will find it hard to work together. Alphas like to do things their own way. But if their partner wants to do something in a different way, then they won't work together, instead they will argue about who's in charge.

The interesting thing about 2 Alphas together in a relationship is that from the outside in they look like a fantastic match in public because Alphas will always keep up a good appearance when around others. This is because their ego doesn't want other people to see their relationship not working. BUT 99% of the time, behind closed doors, it's usually a very different story.

However, despite the lack of compatibility between 2 Alphas in a relationship, they do usually tend to have a good sex life with each other. This is because they both have intense emotions in their day to day lives and these emotions then are usually transferred to their sex lives with each other.

Also 2 Alphas may perceive themselves as a 'Power couple' which they will like because it strokes their egos. However, this novelty wears off after a little while once reality hits.

I don't think I've ever seen 2 TRUE Alphas have a

successful long-term relationship together. Having a good sex life isn't enough to compensate for the inevitable arguing and competition to be the dominant one in the relationship.

Alpha & Beta

This is a very common relationship matchup because both people will naturally fall into their roles within the relationship.

The Alpha will lead, and the Beta will follow.

The Alpha likes to protect, and the Beta likes to feel protected.

The Alpha is decisive, and the Beta is indecisive. So naturally the Alpha will make most of the decisions in the relationship. Both personality types feel comfortable with this arrangement.

The only problem with this type of couple is that if the Alpha has a bad moral compass, they tend to bully the Beta. This is because Betas often avoid conflict which makes them a natural target for bullies. But if it's a nice Alpha who treats their partner the right way, it can be a great match.

Alpha & Sigma

These two personality types usually clash. This is because an Alpha likes to be dominant and in charge, however, you can't try to dominate a Sigma because a Sigma will put them back in their place and dismiss them.

This frustrates many Alphas because it goes against their natural personality because they feel the need to be in charge. Whereas a Sigma hates being told what to do unless they give permission for someone to take the lead, or if it's by somebody more knowledgeable than themselves in the area that they are trying to take the lead (this is usually in a learning capacity, or for a team project).

Sigmas value equality very highly in a relationship, whereas Alphas don't.

Alphas also like to be the protector in a relationship, but because the Sigma is very independently minded, they don't seek the protection of the Alpha. The Alpha doesn't like this because it goes against their natural instincts in a relationship.

Alphas also tend to have a more aggressive communication style, and this is very unappealing to a Sigma.

This makes these 2 personality types very incompatible.

Beta & Sigma

This can be a good match. This is because a Beta will never try to dominate a Sigma, so they will never push them away in that regard.

Also, Betas are usually very friendly and don't like conflict, and this is something a Sigma highly values because even though they can handle conflict well, they don't want the hassle of a conflict.

Sigmas prefer calm discussions over arguments, and because Betas tend to fall into the frame of the other person, if the Sigma is discussing calmly, then the Beta will usually follow the calm demeanour of the Sigma. This way of handling conflicts is healthy because discussions are far better than arguments to handle disagreements.

A Sigma will naturally fall into a leadership role in this type of relationship; however, they won't try to dominate the Beta because their goal is to make the Beta realise they CAN and SHOULD be an equal in the relationship.

Also, because a Sigma values equality above all else, they will help develop a Beta personality type to be more confident within themselves and give them the respect of equality that many Alphas wouldn't.

A Sigma will value their Beta partner's opinions and treat them as an equal; a trait an Alpha usually does not share. Because of this dynamic of the Sigma helping the Beta become more confident, it can be very beneficial and healthy for the Beta personality type.

The only negative thing about this matchup is that Betas tend to need a lot of their partner's affections to feel secure in a relationship. If the Sigma is very emotionally aware of this, and is willing to reassure their partner, then it won't be an issue.

Also, the Beta MUST give the Sigma the alone time that they need and not smother them.

However, Sigma females and Sigma males do respond differently when in a relationship with a Beta...

Sigma males usually have no problem being in a relationship with a Beta female.

However, Sigma females tend to be sexually turned off by Beta males. This is because they don't feel that a Beta male is a strong character because they aren't decisive and they are submissive, and that can be sexually undesirable to a Sigma female. The Sigma female may think the Beta male is a wonderful person, but if that sexual chemistry isn't there then the relationship won't work.

Beta & Beta

This isn't a good match. This is because Betas want to be led. And if no one is taking on a leadership role, then both Betas often feel lost in the relationship.

Also, Betas are usually indecisive characters, and if you have 2 indecisive personalities in a relationship then it doesn't work. Nothing gets done, conflicts don't get settled, there is a lack of planning in the relationship, and much more. It just doesn't work.

When 2 Betas are together, both people feel very frustrated. The relationship won't end in fireworks, but instead, it will more than likely just fizzle out.

Sigma & Sigma

Sigmas are the rarest personality type, so it's very rare to find 2 Sigmas together, however when you do find them together, they work very well. This is because both people have a similar outlook on relationships. Both value equality, both value alone time, both value calmness and peace in the relationship, both are extremely loyal as Sigmas never cheat. It's a great matchup in so many ways.

The only concern for 2 Sigmas in a relationship is that both are lone wolves. They love their alone time, and if they don't make a conscious effort to spend time with each other, then they will get too comfortable being alone, and the relationship will fizzle out. But if they both put in the effort to spend quality time together, then 2 Sigmas together is usually a fantastic matchup.

Which personality types are you and your partner?

Identify which personality type you identify with the most and then assess which personality type your partner is. Once you have done this you will have a better understanding of your relationship and why you work well together, or why you keep having conflict with your partner. This will help you navigate communication with your partner and strengthen your relationship.

Personality types are very interesting and play a major role when dating. Don't underestimate the importance of this chapter.

THE DATING LIFE IN YOUR RELATIONSHIP

When in a relationship you ALWAYS want to keep going on dates each other. One of the biggest mistakes that couples make is that when they get into a relationship, they stop dating each other. So, in this chapter I will be giving you tips and advice on how and why you should keep the dating life in your relationship alive and exciting!

Why you should always go on dates with your partner

I expect when you first met your partner it was fun and exciting. From getting ready and making yourself look at hot as possible for the date, to going home after a fun date and having amazing sex. All of these things are exciting! You may very well love your partner, but you would have also loved the positive emotions associated with going on fun dates. And because of this you must always maintain a healthy dating life together.

The reason why you must always go on regular dates with your partner is because if you don't the relationship becomes very dull and boring. The sex life will become non-existent, and you will start to have arguments.

Why it becomes boring if you don't regularly go on dates

Think about it... It's a Saturday night, and you and your partner don't have anything planned. Instead, you just sit at home doing nothing with your time together...

If you do this every so often it can be great for recharging your energy, but if you do this every weekend, or every day, then your relationship will be very boring and a bit pointless. You will soon run out of things to talk about, and you will start to get on each other's nerves.

The reason this happens is because people get far too comfortable in a relationship and think that all the effort they had to put in at the start of the relationship, such as taking you out on dates etc, doesn't need to be done anymore because they already have you.

It's one of the biggest reasons why I see people break up. Then every single time when the relationship ends, people always wish they had made more of an effort.

Think about it... When you first met and went on fun dates, you had so much to talk about. Regularly going on dates together will build a stronger connection between you both because of the shared experiences that create positive emotions.

But if you just stay at home with your partner 24/7, what is there to talk about and connect over? Not a lot.

Why the sex life will become non-existent if you stop going on dates together

I have no doubt that when you first started dating each other, you two were having a lot of sex.

The reason why is because sex with them was new and exciting. But also, it's not just the act of actually having sex, it's all of the positive emotions leading up to it... Making yourself as hot as possible to impress your partner, the romance, the conversation, everything! This would have got you both sexually charged, and when you got home, you just wanted to rip each other's clothes off and have sex.

But if you stop dating, you are taking away all of those positive things that made you both sexually charged.

Firstly, when you are sat at home not dating, 99% of the time, both of you won't be looking your most attractive and you won't be drooling over each other.

Secondly, there's no connection or emotions being built between you both to get you sexually charged.

And thirdly, when you aren't dating it changes the frame of your relationship into something more platonic and less romantic. It will just be like you're living with a roommate, not your sexual partner, and that's not hot.

When you stop dating, you will start arguing

When people stop regularly dating each other they argue a lot because people's brains need stimulation.

You can have positive stimulation or negative stimulation. We should always strive for positive stimulation. But if people stop dating and stop having good sex, then their brains won't be getting positive stimulation from that person. Instead, they will start trying to get stimulation by other means, aka negative stimulation.

This usually manifests itself in the form of arguments. People start becoming addicted to this type of drama instead of the positive exciting experiences they should be having by doing positive things, such as romantic dates. This is very negative and bad for you and your partner.

Once people start arguing for their stimulation, it then creates a nasty snowball effect. Because you are arguing a lot, the sex life will dry up because stress is one of the biggest killers of your sex drive.

Secondly, you won't want to spend any time around that person because you will start associating them with stress and arguing. Because of this you won't want to go on dates with each other, therefore making everything even worse. Then the outcome will be you both splitting up because the relationship is toxic.

So, it's simple… ALWAYS go on dates with each other.

How often you should go on dates with your partner

Honestly, it's a very simple answer to give. You want to be going on a date with your partner AT LEAST once a week. That is the absolute bare minimum.

I put a post on social media about this and said that you should be going on at least one date a week with your partner and most people agreed. However, there were quite a few people who said that because of their finances they couldn't do that.

If you don't have much money and you think that you need a lot of money to go on dates, then you need to change your mindset.

A date can be anything that you both enjoy. You can spend a lot of money on a date if that's something you want to do; but at the same time, you don't have to spend any money on a date. A date can be something as simple as going for a nice nature walk. (Nature walks are my personal favourite dates).

If you want to go on dates but your partner is saying, 'We can't afford to go on dates', then in my opinion that is just laziness and a lack of creativity and thinking on their part.

Suggest to them going for a nature walk, going for a coffee, or a drink at a cool bar. There are many different options out there that don't cost a lot of money.

However, if they refuse and say 'no', then you will know for a fact that they are using their lack of money as an excuse to be lazy and not go on dates with you. If this is the case, then you need to have a firm conversation with them that you aren't going to stay in a relationship that becomes stale and boring due to laziness on their behalf.

I understand that sometimes once a week might not always be possible as some people have extremely demanding jobs, such as a Doctor who works on the emergency ward, or perhaps a solider who has to be stationed at a certain post; and that is a very good reason to not date once a week as they have more important tasks to complete. However, this isn't the majority of people...

If your partner keeps saying to you, 'I'm busy with work' or 'I just don't have the time', but they don't have an extremely demanding job, then it's just an excuse not to date.

The fact of the matter is that they don't see dating their partner as a priority. This is a real cause for concern in a relationship and will eventually lead to the relationship ending.

Another excuse people make to not go on dates with their partner is because they have children. If you have children and feel like you never have the time to date because you are too busy parenting, do this...

Ask the grandparents to babysit for a few hours whilst you go out. Most grandparents would be willing to do this once every couple of weeks. Or perhaps your friends will babysit if you return the favour for them. Either way, just because you have children, it doesn't mean that you and your partner can't go out on dates together.

Let's say that you have none of these restraints on your dating life. You have money, you don't have an extremely demanding job, and you don't have children, then in my opinion it's very healthy to be going on a date at least twice a week. Once a week is good if you have these restraints.

But again, twice a week if not. If you can do this then I guarantee your relationship will be much stronger than other couples who don't do this.

Take it in turns planning the dates

This is a simple tip that always gets neglected by a lot of couples...

Take it in turns planning the dates. If you plan a date, then it's up to your partner to plan the next one. When you have this mentality and rule in your relationship, you will both be made to feel special and appreciated.

In a relationship where you take it in turns planning the dates, you will both get a sense of giving and receiving in the relationship.

You should be excited to plan a date for your partner and hope that their face lights up with the plans that you made for them.

On the other hand, when it's their turn to plan a date for you, you should be excited in anticipation of what they have planned for you and give yourself to their idea, because they may have put a lot of effort into it. When you are like this, they will be excited to plan a date for you and see your reaction.

Both of you should give yourselves the opportunity to make each other feel wanted, desired, and cared for by taking it in turns to plan the dates.

A lot of relationships have the dynamic of one person always wanting the other person to plan the dates. I think this a selfish mentality from the person who isn't planning the dates. It shows me that they don't really care about their partner feeling wanted and desired.

It also puts a lot of pressure on the person who is making all of the effort and planning the dates. This is a cause for concern if someone has the mentality of 'The other person should plan the dates for me.' It shows that they believe themselves to be superior to their partner, and that's an extremely negative mentality to have and actually shows an abusive mentality.

People should always see their partner as an equal. And as equals, you should treat each other equally.

Spoil each other and I guarantee you will both be much happier in the relationship!

Where to go on dates when in a relationship to keep it EXCITING!

To keep the spark alive in your dating life when in a relationship, there's one simple rule to follow... Have dates that are NEW and EXCITING!

You could go on a date once a week, but if you keep going to the same place EVERY TIME it becomes routine and very boring. You want to keep varying up where you go on a date with your partner. It's ok to revisit places if you have a fun time there. Say for example it's a Wednesday evening and you want to revisit a nice bar to go for a drink, then that's great. But if you do that every time, it gets boring very fast.

So, I'm going to give you some tips on where to go for your dates to keep the spark alive!

Try out new places to eat and drink

Instead of going to a restaurant that you have both been to 10 times before, go to eat somewhere completely different. Perhaps a whole new cuisine! This will give you both something new to talk about as you can talk about the venue, the food, the people that are there etc. And you never know, your favourite place to eat may completely change!

Have competitive dates

Having a competitive date can be very beneficial for your relationship.

A bit of healthy competition can build a lot of sexual tension between you both. For example, if you are playing a game of mini golf, make a fun little bet on it where the winner can request anything they want from the loser...

If you both have a creative mind, you could end up doing some very hot 'activities' after the date.

This builds fun sexual tension and when done regularly it can be very healthy for the relationship.

Have dates where you need to work together

Activities where you need to work together as a team are great because they help you form a stronger bond together. So, there are a few different types of dates where you can do this...

A good example of a date like this is an Escape Room. These are very fun dates where you need to work together to escape. (They aren't as scary as they sound, I promise).

Another great date to make you work as a team is a competitive double date. For example, let's say you invite another couple around to your home and you end up playing a game where it's you and your partner vs the other couple. You will have to work with your partner to beat the other couple at the game. This will make you work together and bring an element of competitiveness to the date. This will build a lot of fun tension between you both which can then be converted into sexual tension once the other couple go home.

Keep both of these types of dates light-hearted and fun and don't get overly competitive where it causes arguments, and it will do wonders for your relationship.

Remember, it's not about winning or losing. It's about having a fun time!

Explore new places

When in a relationship, you always want to be exploring new places with your partner. This can really strengthen your relationship and it's a fun thing to do. Travelling with each other will bring you much closer together.

When you travel you need to work together to navigate where to go, you organise plans with each other, and you get to try new experiences with each other.

If you stay in the same town/city all of the time, your relationship will become very routine and boring. Travel broadens the mind and will help you grow together as a couple.

I always say that a couple that can travel together successfully, and not have arguments, have a strong relationship. So, it's worth doing because travelling will reveal if your relationship is a strong one, or if the relationship is built upon shaky foundations.

Be spontaneous

Sometimes being spontaneous with your dates is a very positive thing to do in your relationship.

What I mean by this is... Let's say you don't have anything planned for that day with your partner, but then out of nowhere the mood strikes you to go on a date. Then you pick a random spontaneous date to go on. This will make you both feel that the relationship is fresh and exciting.

Sometimes randomly book that night away with your partner for no reason at all other than you just want to surprise them. They will love this and will always be bragging to their friends about how spontaneous and exciting their partner can be...

What to do if your partner doesn't want to go on dates

This is a common occurrence that happens in many relationships. There are a couple of ways to handle this to get your dating life with your partner back on track...

1. Ask them why they don't want to go on dates.

This may sound like an obvious answer, however lots of people won't ask because they are worried about starting an argument. But if you don't ask, you'll never know.

They may be worried about spending money. If this is the case, suggest going on a date that costs little to no money.

Perhaps they are overly tired from being over worked. If this is the case, then suggest to them solutions on how they can better manage their time.

Some people may say they don't want to go on a date with you because you two have been arguing regularly. If this is the case, sometimes going on a date is the BEST idea. It's gets you both out of the house and into a different environment with each other. This will get you away from the same environment where you have both been arguing.

Whatever their answer to 'Why don't you want to go on dates?' is, offer them a solution to help them overcome this dating barrier of theirs. And if they still aren't willing to go on dates, then it's a good indicator that something else is wrong in the relationship...

2. Choose a Date Day for the week and stick to it.

Having a day each week that is allocated for you to spend time together will bring you closer together. It ensures you both make time for each other and make the other person feel like a priority.

For example, let's say that your Date Day is a Sunday, then a friend asked you to see them instead, and then you decline their offer... By doing this you are showing your partner that your relationship is a priority to you and it will make them feel wanted and desired. This will strengthen your relationship so much more. It's a simple tip but it works wonders for your relationship.

Now, let's say that they always bail and cancel on Date Day, then you know for a fact it's not about them finding the time to date, it's a matter of them NOT wanting to go on a date with you. If this is the case, then you need to ask yourself if you want to be in a relationship where you don't feel like a priority.

HOW TO MAKE YOUR PARTNER FEEL LOVED

When we truly love someone, we want them to feel and know how loved they are. Some people are fantastic at this, whereas some people find it a little harder to express their love for their partner in a healthy way…

Sometimes people love their partner but just don't know how to express it.

Sometimes they don't know their partner's needs and wants in a relationship.

Sometimes they have never been shown love themselves, so they don't know how to show someone else their love for them, because they've had no examples of how to express love for someone else in a healthy way.

In this chapter I will be giving you advice and guidance on how you can make your partner feel loved in your relationship ...

Learn your partner's wants and needs

This tip is very simple. Sometimes all you need to do is ask someone what they want and need from you in a relationship. Sometimes it could be something that you would have never expected, but it means the world to them, and it could be something super simple and easy for you to do.

Another way of learning what your partner wants is by surprising them by introducing new things into the relationship. The things they want and enjoy may change when they are introduced to new things, and I'm sure they'll appreciate the effort you put in for them.

Give your partner compliments & words of affirmation

Your words are very powerful. Your words can make your partner feel loved, and a lack of words can make them feel unloved. Many people forget to compliment and give words of affirmation to their partner because they expect their partner to know how they feel, but that isn't always the case.

Always remember to compliment your partner. If they look good, tell them. If they have done something good, thoughtful, intelligent etc, tell them how proud of them you are. These compliments will go a long way.

I'm a firm believer that you and your partner should always be complimenting each other and being each other's biggest cheerleader in life. Not many people receive compliments throughout their day, but when they come home to their partner who does compliment them, it will make coming home the favourite part of their day, and they will feel loved and appreciated.

Always remember to tell your partner that you love them. Do this regularly. When they go to work, tell them you love them. End a phone call with 'I love you'. Before you go to sleep, tell them you love them.

If you both compliment and give each other words of affirmation throughout your relationship, you'll have a much happier and healthier relationship.

Listen when your partner is expressing their feelings

This is one of the most bare minimum things you can do for your partner, yet it's something that many people don't do in their relationships. Listen to your partner when they are expressing their feelings.

There are few things that will end a relationship faster than when one person doesn't listen to their partner expressing themselves.

If your partner is sad, listen. If they are frustrated, listen. If they are confused, listen.

Once you take the time to hear your partner expressing themselves, you can then act accordingly and address what your partner is feeling, and if needed, you can help them come up with a solution to any problems they are having.

On the other hand, also listen to them when they are expressing positive emotions. If they are excited by something that means a lot to them, listen to why it makes them excited and display genuine interest in what they have to say.

If you are in a disagreement with your partner, let them have their time to talk and listen without interrupting. This will make them feel like an equal. Even if you are in the right during a disagreement, if you listen to what they have to say, you are a lot more likely to understand how they have come to their conclusions, and then you can act accordingly to what they have said and tell them why they are wrong in a way that they will understand.

When you both take the time to allow each other to express what you are feeling, the relationship will develop greatly because you will know how each other thinks and feels.

Take an interest in your partner's life outside of the relationship

It's great when you both have your own lives and don't solely rely upon each other to pass the time. And it's also great when you take a genuine interest in each other's lives outside of your relationship.

For example, when they come home from doing their hobby, ask them how it went and listen to them. It may sound small, but they will massively appreciate this.

Take an interest in their friends. If they come home after spending time with friends, ask them how their friends are doing. This shows that you care about the different relationships they have outside of your own relationship with them. It will also make them feel comfortable to integrate you into their social circle because they won't feel any negative friction or separation between you and their friends.

Also, when you two are together you will have more to talk about because you know more about each other's lives, and you can both add more value and understanding to the conversation.

Acts of service in your relationship

Acts of service are very important in a relationship. Going out of your way and doing things for your partner will show them how much you care for them.

This can be things as simple as:

- Doing an extra chore when they are busy to take a little bit of stress out of their life.

- Giving them a massage after they've had a hard day at work.

- Making them their favourite food.

- Planning a surprise date for your partner.

There's a million different ways you can show your partner your love for them by doing little acts of service that will make them happy.

Regularly doing these little things for each other will go a long way in strengthening your relationship.

Give your partner reassurance when they need it

Sometimes we all get a little insecure and need our partner to reassure us. It's perfectly normal.

For example, if your partner is feeling a bit insecure that you aren't attracted to them, you need to reassure them that you are (assuming you are).

- Ask them why they feel this way.

- What triggered it?

- Was it something that you have done to make them feel this way?

- Is it something from their past that makes them feel unattractive?

Ask them these types of questions and listen to what they have to say. Then once they have told you, you can reassure them.

Address the things that triggered these emotions.

Let them know you do find them attractive and make sure to be kind and reassuring in your delivery.

Another example could be if your partner is scared that you're going to leave them because they don't feel good enough. Again, ask them questions why they feel like this and reassure them that you aren't going to leave them (if you aren't planning on leaving them of course).

HOWEVER, there does come a point when reassuring someone too much can be more damaging than good because they will form a co-dependency with you because they aren't addressing their own anxieties. Instead, they are using you to ease their anxieties instead of having the self-confidence to reassure themselves.

If it becomes excessive where they are constantly asking you to reassure them at every chance they get, then you need to address their concerns in a different way. If it's not the usual insecurities many people have in a relationship, but instead, it's a deeper anxiety that needs to be dealt with, that's not always something you can help with.

For example, if they have been cheated on in their past relationship, they will naturally feel insecure that you may cheat on them because it has happened to them before and it deeply hurt them. Then they may become very unsure of your relationship because they are projecting their emotions associated with their past relationship on to you, and that isn't fair on you.

But if you overly reassure them to the point where it becomes highly excessive, then you aren't allowing them to overcome this anxiety themselves. If their anxiety is badly affecting them, then I highly suggest they talk to a therapist who can address the root causes of their anxieties and help them overcome it.

Make time for each other

Please make time for each other. This is such an easy thing to do, yet so many people don't do it. I understand that life can become very busy, but please don't ignore the ones you love.

One of the most important things you have in your life is your relationships with others. When you are on your death bed you aren't going to be wishing you spent more time at work, or watched more TV etc; but instead, you would have wished you spent more time with your loved ones.

I want you and your partner to do this... Sit down and plan at least one day of the week that is just for you two. Spend the whole day with each other. Go on a date, try something new, fully engage with each other. I promise you that this will strengthen your relationship much more than people realise. If you have kids together then get a babysitter one evening of the week and go on a date together.

But it doesn't always have to be about going on a date with each other... When you are at home, don't sit on your phones ignoring each other. Instead...

- You can cook together

- Have deep conversations

- Play a fun game together

- Get out the popcorn, build a comfy nest and have movie night

I promise you that you won't regret it.

Let's say that one, or both of you have demanding jobs and you don't feel like you can make time for each other... If this is the case, then you need to plan out your schedules in a way where you CAN make time for each other.

You don't want to be working so much that you neglect your relationship. What would be the point of building your career if you can't share the rewards with those you love? Seems pointless to me.

There are many people who have excelled in their career,

work lots of hours, and make a lot of money, but they aren't happy people. The reason is because they haven't got anyone to share their success with.

You don't have to put your whole life into building your career. There should be a balance in your life otherwise it will damage the relationships you have with people; and if you don't make time for those closest to you, you'll end up alone.

But when you actively make the choice to make time for your partner, and they can see this, they will feel loved and appreciated because you are showing them that they are a priority to you.

Keep working on yourself

One of the best ways that you can show your partner that you love them is by constantly working on yourself. This is something many people overlook in a relationship. You want your partner to always be attracted to you, proud of you, and feel inspired by you.

For example, keep your body healthy. Eat clean, exercise, live a healthy lifestyle. This will make you as attractive as possible for your partner. They will greatly appreciate this.

Let's say that one of you is constantly improving their physical appearance whereas the other person doesn't bother at all... Well, it's not going to be an equal relationship if this is the case.

The person who makes no effort on their appearance will have a super hot partner, however the person who does make an effort won't have a partner who is actively trying to make themselves as attractive as possible for them. It's not fair and will do damage to the relationship.

Another example is when someone works on their intellect.

Let's say that one of you puts effort into building their knowledge by reading, learning new skills, challenging themselves, BUT the other person doesn't bother doing these things... Well, I guarantee that relationship will fail because you won't be on the same wavelength anymore. But if you BOTH keep learning new things, your relationship will thrive, and you'll achieve amazing things together.

I've seen many relationships where one person works on building their knowledge and the other person doesn't, and they always break up because the person who works on building up their knowledge ends up getting bored and frustrated with their partner, and leaves to find someone else who is better suited for them.

So, if both of you keep working on yourselves, you will both grow together and achieve great things together. You'll both be very attracted to each other for all the right reasons, and that's exactly what you want. But if one of you gets lazy, then that relationship will fail...

Let them have their alone time

Many arguments happen in relationships because one person doesn't respect that the other person wants their alone time to relax and decompress. Some people need their alone time to be happy, and that's ok.

For example, many couples argue about video games. Someone in the relationship enjoys playing video games, whilst the other person doesn't want them to play it because they want their partner's attention.

I understand both people's perspectives when it comes to this situation, but it's all about compromising with each other in this scenario...

Let them play their video games if it helps them to relax and decompress. However, they must meet you in the middle and prioritise spending quality time with you and not play their video games an excess amount. Once you both meet in the middle, you will both feel much happier.

Another example is sometimes people need to relax when they come home from work. Some people simply want to make themselves a nice cup of tea or coffee and chill out in front of the TV or relax on their phone for a bit, so they can zone out and relax from a stressful day.

This is also an acceptable thing to do, and the other person must respect their choice to relax this way. However, there must be a compromise in this scenario...

When they come home, they must acknowledge you and ask how you are etc before their alone time. This only takes a few minutes of their time and will mean a lot to the other person.

Some people love spending time alone and doing a certain activity. This could be going to the gym, a hobby of theirs, perhaps they like to go for walks alone etc. This is something that the other person in the relationship must respect and accept. If they don't allow their partner to do this and demand all of their attention, it will destroy the relationship because the other person will be feeling pressurised and suffocated in the relationship.

Honestly, just allowing them to have their alone

time uninterrupted will do amazing things for your relationship. You are showing your partner you respect their space and that's very important to making your partner feel respected and loved by you. It will strengthen your bond and make you crave each other much more. BUT, like I said, TOO MUCH alone time isn't good. Just be sure to make time for each other and have a healthy balance of alone time and quality time together...

ARGUMENTS

A lot of couples accept that regular arguments are simply something that comes with being in a relationship… But let me tell you this… IT'S NOT! An argument here and there is something that will always happen, but REGULAR arguments is something that SHOULDN'T be happening.

What's most important is how you handle arguments. Many relationships end because people handle arguments the wrong way. A lot of people have never been taught how to handle arguments in relationships, but in this chapter, I'm going to teach you how to navigate arguments the CORRECT way.

If you follow the advice in this chapter, I guarantee that when an argument occurs in your relationship, it will be much easier to handle. Let's get into it…

Who's fault is it?

Ok, so one of the most common reasons for arguments is confusion as to who is in the wrong. However, if you follow the rules that I am about to tell you, then it's much easier to tell who is in the wrong and who needs to apologise...

The 3 Rules of 'Who is in the wrong'

Rule 1.
If your instructions of what you want are UNCLEAR and somebody doesn't do what you want, then YOU are at fault. But if your instructions are CLEAR and easy to understand, and they do something different, then it is THEIR fault.

Example:
If you said to your partner, 'I guess it's ok if you like other women's pictures on social media', then you get angry at them because they like other women's pictures, then technically they haven't really done anything wrong. This is because you said it's 'ok'.

But if you said to them, 'I don't like it when you like other women's pictures on social media', and then they still do it, then they are completely in the wrong because you have CLEARLY said that you don't like it.

Sidenote: In my opinion, he shouldn't go around liking other random women's pictures on social media anyway. This is something you shouldn't need to tell him. But I'm just using this as an example for this rule as this is a conversation many couples have.

Rule 2.
Consider what the other person's intentions are behind their actions. If they had GOOD intentions but did something wrong, then it was an ACCIDENT and must be treated as one. However,

if they had BAD intentions with whatever they have done towards you, the argument is their fault.

Example:
If your partner makes a joke and they thought that you would find it funny, but unfortunately it ends up upsetting you, then as long as they apologise and don't repeat their behaviours then it's ok because they didn't have any bad intentions.

However, if your partner says something to you with the intention to hurt or upset you, then they are 100% at fault.

Rule 3.
If they are REPEATING negative behaviours that lead to arguments, it's their fault.

Example:
Your partner keeps making a mess around the house and leaves it up to you to tidy up after them... If you have told them it upsets you and they keep repeating this behaviour and it leads to an argument, then it is entirely their fault.

Conclusion:

Next time you are in an argument, and you are both playing the blame game, I want you to stop and think about these 3 rules. This way you should be able to determine who is in the wrong and needs to apologise and change their behaviour.

Admit when you are wrong

Many arguments in relationships could be easily resolved if people just admitted when they are wrong.

Throughout my whole life I have witnessed so many people do wrong YET still argue their case even when they have been proven wrong. This is because their EGO won't accept that they are wrong. It's a very immature perspective to still argue a case even when you have been proven wrong.

If every time you and your partner argue and your partner is letting their ego get carried away, then you need to remove yourself from the situation because it's very hard to debate and reason with someone who has a big ego.

Instead, tell them that they are letting their ego and their need to be right ruin the relationship. And if they value your relationship, they will correct their behaviour.

Also, people won't admit they are wrong, even when they are, because they want to feel superior over someone else at all costs. This is a very toxic behaviour and extremely damaging to a relationship.

If someone always needs to feel superior in arguments, then it's near enough impossible for that relationship to grow.

Firstly, the other person will never feel heard.

Secondly, the person with the superiority complex will never learn from their mistakes.

Thirdly, it shows the person who needs to feel superior doesn't care about or value the other person's feelings.

If your partner is like this and they won't change their

ways even when you have expressed how it makes you feel, then you need to reassess if you want to be in a relationship with this person or not. This is because these sorts of behaviours can lead to even more malicious and sinister behaviours. I've seen it happen many times. Don't be with someone who feels they MUST feel superior over you.

Don't turn it into a shouting match

When having an argument, many people turn it into shouting matches, and this is NEVER productive at getting your point across. Just because we speak louder, it doesn't add any value to what we are saying. Instead, it just makes the other person want to shout as well, or somebody ends up crying etc. If you are ever in this position where either of you feel like you are raising your voices, I want you to do this...

Take a step back and pause. Relax your body, mind, and voice, and think to yourself, 'Is what I am saying constructive or is there a better choice of words I could use to get my point across?' Then once you feel that you have a better choice of words to communicate what you want to say, then talk to your partner again using these better words.

Once you both start thinking with this mindset your relationship will become much easier because you will be having discussions instead of arguments. You'll also be able to truly understand each other and come to solutions instead of conflicts.

Your partner always finds it funny to annoy you and it causes a lot of arguments

This is a fascinating topic when you delve into it. Humour can be a very good thing to have in relationships. Teasing each other can be fun and having at laugh at each other can strengthen the bond. HOWEVER, how much and WHEN one indulges in humour is important...

Ok, so one of the age-old questions is, 'What is humour?'...

When we find something funny it's usually from us feeling superior over someone. This doesn't have to have a sinister undertone to it, providing it's done in the correct way.

For example, if your partner is having some food and they get a bit on their nose, it can be funny...

The reason why our brains would find this funny is because it's embarrassing for the other person. And if they feel embarrassed around us, we feel superior over that person and our brain responds by finding it funny as a reward system for ourselves.

So, if you can both laugh at each other for these sorts of things then that's absolutely fine because it's just our human nature and no one's feelings are getting properly hurt.

HOWEVER, remember this... If someone's feelings get truly hurt, then you shouldn't find it funny. You should care enough about your partner that your brain's feelings of empathy and respect for them overrides any feelings of humour that you may have.

BUT, if someone is ALWAYS trying to make fun of you, it's usually because they have a superiority/inferiority complex. They want you to feel bad, and when you do feel bad, they feel superior over you and their brain rewards them with the feeling of finding it funny. Think of someone who is a bully… They always pick on someone and laugh at them. And ALL bullies have a serious superiority/inferiority complex.

If your partner is someone who always tries making fun of you to the point that it upsets you, then explain very clearly and precisely why it upsets you. If they stop their negative behaviours, then ok. BUT if they respond in a negative way and continue their negative behaviour, then they care more about feeling superior over you than they do about your feelings. Don't stay with someone who doesn't respect your feelings.

Not repeating the behaviours is the best apology

This piece of advice is simple… The best apology is NOT repeating the same behaviour.

I get it… People in life make mistakes, and many mistakes are forgivable. HOWEVER, if that person keeps repeating their mistakes, then it's not just a 'mistake', it's a choice.

My father had a good saying when I was growing up and it was, 'Once is a mistake, twice is on purpose.' And I agree with this quote for most of the time. However, there are exceptions when learning new things, as its natural to make the same mistakes a few times, but there are NO exceptions at all when it comes to disrespectful behaviour.

So, let's say your partner has done something disrespectful to you such as, they always make a mess in the kitchen and never clean up after themselves and always expect you to do it…

This could be because they never had proper parenting growing up and never learnt how to tidy up after themselves. Or perhaps, for example, their father always made their mother clean up and they witnessed this and thought it was normal behaviour (which it isn't). Or they may just be a lazy and selfish person. No matter what the reason is, I want you to do this…

Say to them, 'You must clean up after yourself because I'm not your parent. It's disrespectful to me that you expect me to clean up after you, and it shows that you don't think very highly of me. I am not your servant and won't be doing it again. Clean up after yourself next time.'

If they apologise and do clean up after themselves after this conversation, that's great. It was a mistake that they won't repeat. You can't ask for much more than that…

However, if they carry on leaving the kitchen in a mess and expect you to clean up after them, then it's completely disrespectful to you. You then need to be very firm with them and say that you aren't willing to stay in a relationship with someone who disrespects you.

If they STILL don't clean up after themselves, then you need to think about if you want to stay in a relationship where someone is repeatedly disrespecting you.

Once people have been shown their mistakes and taught how not to repeat them, but they still continue to do so, then there's no hope for this type of person to have a healthy relationship and you need to reconsider if they are the right person for you. But if they choose the path of correcting their mistakes, that's great!

It's how you react that matters

This is so true. In life we can't always control what happens to us, however we can ALWAYS control how we choose we react.

Let's say your partner has done something incredibly stupid, disrespectful, or unkind to you, then that's not your fault. BUT how you choose to react to that situation is your fault whether it be for the good or the bad. Just because somebody else is being an idiot, it doesn't mean that you must be one as well.

Let's say your partner has said something hurtful to you... A common reaction many people have is to say something hurtful back. But when you do this, you are no better than them and they have become your master because they have influenced your emotions in a negative way, and you have fallen into their frame.

However, if your partner says something hurtful to you and you don't engage in conversation with them and simply remove yourself from the situation, their disrespect and anger fully becomes their own and has nothing to do with you. You walk away the bigger and more peaceful person.

Another example could be... Let's say that your partner says to you that they don't feel loved or desired in your relationship... You now have 2 choices...

1. You can ignore them and change nothing, resulting in making them feel unloved and undesired.

2. You can make a big effort to make your partner feel loved

and desired again.

The situation hasn't changed, but the way you react to the situation will change the course of your relationship either for the better or for the worse.

Throughout your whole relationship you will be presented with lots of different scenarios, but how you react to these scenarios is what truly matters. Always make the right choice and you will have a much happier relationship.

What to do if your partner won't listen to you

This is always an unfortunate situation to be in. No matter what you say, your partner just won't listen to you, and they always think that they are right, and you are wrong, and they think they know everything in the world.

These types of people ALWAYS struggle in relationships. But there comes a point in your relationship where you need to ask yourself, 'Why am I with somebody who doesn't listen to me?'

Listening is one of the most basic skills of communication that even children can do. And if your partner, who is a full-grown adult, can't or refuses to listen to you, then to me it shows that they are disrespectful and have no room for self-development and personal growth in their lives. This is NOT the type of person you want to be in a relationship with.

It also indicates that they think they are superior to you if they never listen to what you have to say.

If this happens between you and your partner on a regular basis, then ask yourself if you want to be in this type of relationship… I expect the answer is ‘No’.

Don’t say words that you can’t take back

This is definitely something that many people need to hear. ‘Don’t say words that you can’t take back.’

When emotions are at a high point, many people act impulsively and blurt out the first thing that comes to their minds. And once a word has been said, it can’t be unsaid. Also, most of the time, it’s the wrong thing to say and it escalates the argument even further and can be very hurtful and damaging to the relationship.

So, this piece of advice is easy… Before you say something in an argument, take your time and think to yourself, ‘I am saying EXACTLY what I am trying to communicate, or am I letting my emotions control me?’ Thinking like this will save yourself and your partner from so much hassle and stress in your relationship.

Your partner always needs to have the last word

Have you ever argued with someone, and they always need to have the last word? I expect the answer is ‘yes’! It’s very frustrating because even when the argument is finished, they need to say just one more little thing, and this behaviour comes from a bad place.

People who MUST have the last word during every

argument do it because they need to feel superior over their partner. They do it to control the frame. And they think if they control the frame, they control you.

The fact of the matter is, that the argument was more of a superiority competition to them, instead of working as a team and resolving the argument.

Next time you and your partner argue pay close attention to if they need to have the last word. Make a conscious effort to finish the argument and see if they say something under their breath, or even directly to you after you've finished talking. If they do then you know that they don't see you as an equal, but instead, someone they need to feel superior over.

If they do need to ALWAYS have the last word in an argument, point out that behaviour to them and explain what it means.

Now here's the interesting part... If they reflect on their behaviour and realise that's what they are doing and then apologise, that's great. It could simply have been a learnt behaviour from their past because they felt inferior to others.

Obviously, someone must have the last word in an argument, but as long as it's not them every time, like before, then that's healthy progress.

On the other hand, if their behaviours don't change and they still always need to have the last word, it shows they care more about feeling superior over you instead of wanting to resolve the argument with you as a team.

Why going on a 'break' won't fix your relationship problems

When relationships come across tough times, many people will take a break from the relationship... I don't think that I have ever witnessed a couple take a break and then come back and have a happy relationship. It just doesn't work that way. **You are rescheduling your arguments, not resolving them**.

Think about it, what will taking a break from each other actually accomplish?

Perhaps the emotions will calm down and you can both come back into the relationship in a calmer manner...

HOWEVER, 99% of the time, you will go back to arguing with each other because the same problems will arise. This is because if you have a break from each other but don't take the time to learn how to communicate more effectively with each other, then the break was a waste of time and you're just prolonging the relationship ending.

I believe if you are in an argument with each other and there seems to be no end to it insight because both of you aren't understanding how to communicate effectively, then you BOTH must approach the argument in a very different manner.

Instead, just have a day of thinking to yourself, 'How can I reapproach our disagreement in a way that is calm, and in a way where we can better understand each other?' Then once you have a better way to reapproach the disagreement in your mind, then talk to your partner about the topic again.

This is a much healthier approach to any disagreement.

CONTROLLING BEHAVIOURS IN A RELATIONSHIP

If you are in a relationship and you feel that your partner is trying to control you, it can be a terrible position to find yourself in. Nobody should be trying to control anyone in a relationship.

In this chapter I am going to be talking about:

- Examples of controlling behaviours.

- Why people have these controlling behaviours.

- What you should do if your partner is trying to control you.

So, if you are in a controlling relationship, I highly recommend reading this chapter. If you allow these controlling behaviours from your partner to continue,

I guarantee that it will develop into even more severe abusive behaviours in the future...

They try to isolate you away from your friends and family

Having a partner that isolates you away from your friends and family is a terrible partner to have. This is a very common behaviour amongst abusive people.

Your friends and family are your lifeline because they will have your best interests in their minds, and they can view your relationship from an outward perspective. This is incredibly important because when you are in a relationship your emotions can cloud your judgement about what is really going on in the relationship. But an outsider can see exactly what is going on. Abusive people are aware of this, and they will try to get you away from your friends and family as much as possible, so you become easier for them to control, manipulate, and abuse.

For example, if your partner is being abusive physically or emotionally and your friends/family are aware of it, then they would intervene and come to save you. But if you have cut off communication from your friends and family, and you are being abused, then nobody would know about it. This is why an abuser will take you away from your friends/family.

If your partner is trying to isolate you away from everyone close to you, LEAVE that relationship immediately. I promise you that the longer you take to leave them, the harder it will become, because abusers will try to make you dependent upon them, so it gets harder for you to leave them over time.

Don't try to compromise with your partner if they are like this, because you won't change them. Take my advice and leave before it's too late. This abusive behaviour of theirs is just the beginning of something far more sinister.

They try telling you what you can or can't wear

It's usually more common for men to try to control what clothes women wear, however some women do try to control what clothes men wear. The most common reason why people do this is because they don't want their partner to look attractive to other people.

People behave this way because of their own insecurities. They can't handle other people looking at you. They think that if someone else finds you attractive, they may try to flirt with you, then you flirt back and end up leaving your partner for them.

Basically, they feel inferior to other people because they lack confidence within themselves; so, they try to control how you look so you don't look as attractive to other people. And in their mind, this eliminates any potential competition they have.

If your partner is like this, you need to handle it in this way...

Say to them, 'Don't tell me what I can or can't wear. I will wear whatever I like, and if you don't like it, then that's your problem. If you try to control what I'm wearing ever again then I am leaving you.'

Only give them one warning!

If you comply to their demands and you wear what they want you to wear, they will start trying to control other aspects of your life, and you don't want to be involved with someone like that.

High value, confident people will like it that you look attractive in public because they like to show you off to the world, and they are confident within themselves that you won't leave them.

They tell you when you can or can't go out

I'll make this as simple as possible... If you want to go out and see your friends, then go out and see your friends! The only thing you need to be aware of is if you constantly see your friends and neglect spending time with your partner, resulting in your partner feeling lonely in the relationship.

The responsibility would fall on you to recognise that you are not spending enough time with your partner. BUT if you have been spending quality time with your partner, then there is nothing holding you back from seeing your friends as much as you want.

They may not want you seeing your friends because they want to isolate you away from other people, so you are easier for them to manipulate, so they can perform other abusive behaviours. And if that is the case, leave them instantly.

The other reason is because they are scared you may talk to other people. This stems from their own insecurities. BUT this is never an excuse for them to try and control you.

Sit down and have a conversation with them and find out if it's because they feel insecure within themselves and if they are worried about you talking to other people and leaving them for someone else...

If it is, give them 1 warning telling them that you will see your friends whenever you want and reassure them that you will spend quality time with them as well, but you need to have your own life and see your friends.

If they apologise and never repeat this behaviour, then give them 1 more chance. HOWEVER, if they keep repeating this behaviour, leave them because nobody should be trying to control you.

Whenever you go out with your friends, your partner should tell you to have a great time... But remember, you need to spend time with your partner AND friends to have a healthy social life and a healthy relationship.

They try to control you with money

It's super important that you have control of your own finances.

If your partner is telling you:

- What you can or can't do with your money

- Giving you an allowance

- Expecting you to do things for them because they pay for you

... Be very careful because you are heading down a disastrous road.

For example, if you live with your partner, and they have

control of all the money between you both, when you want to buy something, you will have to ask your partner if you can go and buy the thing that you wanted...

They have made you ask for their permission to buy something like a child would ask their parent. This isn't healthy at all! They've created a dynamic where you aren't equals in the relationship. Instead, they will feel superior to you. This behaviour creeps into other areas of your relationship. They will become more demanding, forceful and expect more from you when they demand it. Give people a little power and they will get carried away.

Another example is if they give you an allowance. Think about it... They can tell you exactly what you can spend per month. That isn't freedom in a relationship. Your relationship isn't a job. It should be something loving between 2 people. Because they are giving you an allowance, they have a lot of control over your life, and that's no way to live.

The easiest solution to this is to have your own source of income. This way you are always protecting yourself and aren't allowing anyone to have any control over your finances because you are financial independent and don't need their money. And if they try to control what you do with YOUR money, then leave them because a healthy minded person wouldn't want to control what you do with your own money.

However, let's say that you are a stay-at-home parent, and your partner works full-time and makes the income... If this is the case, you need to approach the matter the correct way, so everyone is happy. Please head to the chapter titled 'Money' to see how to handle different situations when it comes to finances, so you and your partner handle the dynamic of finances in a relationship the correct way.

As a full-grown adult, nobody should have control over your finances but YOU.

They try to force their religious, cultural, or political views upon you

There is nothing more annoying than someone who forces their points of view upon you. It's damaging to someone's mentality when they are forced to think a certain way when they don't feel like that.

Everyone is entitled to their own opinions on religion, culture and politics and everyone's views should be respected. (As long as the views aren't extreme to the point where they harm people).

If your partner doesn't respect your views on these different aspects of your life and try to force you to think in another way, then you need to set extremely firm boundaries with them and tell them to respect your views, the same way you respect theirs. If they can't accept that, then it's time to leave the relationship.

Many individuals in couples have different views on religion, culture, and politics, but all of the happiest couples respect each other's different views and don't try to force their partner to change the way they think. Instead, they love them for who they are, and they wouldn't try to change them.

They try to control you be destroying your self-confidence

A devious person will try to control you by destroying your

self-confidence over time.

They will make it appear to others as if they don't control you because they won't be directly telling you what to do. Instead, they will make it so you will be so unsure of yourself that you will feel the need to ask for their opinion or approval to do things or even think a certain way, and this makes it appear that they are helping you out. But in reality, they are the ones who made you dependent upon them in the first place. It's a very devious and evil way of manipulating someone.

You may be asking, 'How do they do this?'... I'm going to tell you how...

From the very start of your relationship, they will subtly attack your confidence by constantly questioning your choices and telling you why your choices are wrong. Then eventually they will start saying things, such as, 'You're stupid' and other words of that nature. This way you will slowly start to doubt yourself.

This way of slowly attacking your confidence could happen in many areas of your life, such as your fashion choices, how you handle social situations, your money choices etc.

Now, let's say you are someone who has good fashion, and you wear attractive clothing... If someone is insecure, they won't like that because they don't like other people looking at you.

So, instead of saying, 'Don't wear that', they will say things like, 'Are you sure you should be wearing that? I think that sort of clothing isn't very flattering on you. Would you like me to help you choose something to wear because I don't think you know what you are doing.'

What they are saying may sound rude, but if you are a little unconfident in yourself, then you may fall for it if they deliver their critique with a soft caring tone in their voice.

Then when you wear unattractive clothing, they will shower you in praise and reinforce your behaviours to suit their own wants. Then whenever you wear clothing that they don't like, they will punish you by either being dismissive towards you or critiquing your choices again.

Be aware if your partner is like this to you. Your partner should help you feel more confident in life, not less confident. Don't stay with someone who takes your confidence away!

Compliance Testing

Compliance Testing is when someone will start off small and under the radar by asking you to do things that you wouldn't even think of saying 'no' to, so it gets you used to saying 'yes' to them.

This is their way of conditioning your brain to be more agreeable to their demands. Then over time they ask you for bigger and more demanding things that you would have said 'no' to before and expect you to be more likely to do it because they have conditioned you to say 'yes' to them.

This is how you see people end up doing things that we think are absurd and unthinkable. It's because over time they have agreed to do little things for that person, and it's been built up over time to become bigger and more challenging demands.

However, not all compliance testing is bad. Sometimes it's

a good thing...

For example, when talking to someone new, if you ask for a date instantly it would be considered a little forward and most people would say 'no'. But if you talk a bit, ask them to put their number into your phone, then ask them to call you one night when they are free, then ask them for a date, they are more likely to say 'yes' to the date because they have complied with you before by giving you their number and giving you a phone call. So, in that regards it's not an evil thing, it's a normal thing to do.

It all comes down to if someone has good intentions or bad intentions.

But like I said, if used by a bad person for bad purposes it can be a very slippery slope into them being able to control you and getting you to do some things you wouldn't have dreamed of doing.

So how do you know if you've had someone doing 'compliance testing' on you?

Look at your behaviour and think...

- Have I ever done things that I never would have said 'yes' to before, but now I do because this person asks me to?

- When they asked me to do something, did it feel uncomfortable to say 'yes' to, but I still did it anyway?

- Are they dismissive to me if I say 'no' to them?

- Do they pressure me into saying 'yes'? And when I do say 'yes', are they nice to me again and reinforce my compliant behaviour?

If you answered 'yes' to any of these questions I've just asked you, then chances are they have been doing 'compliance testing' on you all along and that's how you ended up doing things you never thought you would have.

Some people are clever and calculated and know that they are doing compliance testing on you.

However, some people aren't aware of what they are doing but have done this behaviour from a very young age and have gotten the results they've wanted, so they continue to do this in their adult life.

If you feel like your partner has done compliance testing on you, set very firm boundaries so this doesn't happen again.

If they get angry when you say 'no' to them after they've asked you to do something unreasonable, then distance yourself away from this person. They are not a good person, and you shouldn't be with someone who makes you do things you don't want to do.

PHONES

The phone can be a big topic of conversation in many relationships. I believe you can tell a lot about how someone is in a relationship by the way they are on their phone. I have yet to be proven wrong by this.

So, in this chapter I am going to be giving you some easy rules for you and your partner to follow when it comes to how you both navigate communication over the phone with each other...

How fast your partner should respond to you on the phone

There is nothing more annoying than when you message somebody and you need an answer from them, yet they take forever to reply. It causes so many arguments.

If your partner is at work or genuinely busy and they don't reply, then that's ok because they have a legit excuse. Or even if they are super tired and want an evening alone to decompress and they communicate that to you, then that's also ok if they aren't as responsive.

However, if they don't have a legitimate reason to not be answering you, it can be very disrespectful. I'm not saying you must be on the phone with each other 24/7, but I am saying that they should reply when you need them to.

Let's say that your partner and you have arranged to see each other in 3 days... Then it comes to the day of you two seeing each other, yet you need to know the exact time to meet, where to meet etc, and you are texting them asking them for this information and they don't respond...

Well in my opinion, it's a clear display of disrespect towards you. This is because they don't care about you being stressed and confused. Instead, they are more concerned about whatever they are doing instead of how you feel. It's just plain rude and as an adult they should know how to use their phone properly. When they do this, it also shows a low value behaviour on their behalf because they don't know how to arrange the simplest of things.

So, it's simple... Be responsive when your partner needs a response, and you will avoid a lot of arguments.

Why you shouldn't go through your partner's phone without their permission

This happens A LOT in many relationships. People start searching through their partners phones and it creates a relationship full of distrust and anxiety.

Ok, I get it... If you think your partner is cheating, you will naturally become extremely curious about what is on their phone to see if your suspicions have been right all along. This is the one of the main reasons why people look through their partner's phone.

But once you do look through their phone, you must know that there is no coming back from it. Once it's done you will forever be known for crossing that boundary that you looked through their phone, and that's something you can't take back.

If your suspicions are proved to be correct, then ok, you found out they were cheating, and you can then leave them. However, if your suspicions were incorrect, then you are going to look very silly and distrusting of your partner when they did nothing wrong at all, and that's going to greatly damage the relationship.

What I suggest is this...

If you think they are cheating on you, don't go through their phone. Instead confront them about it and tell them why you think they are cheating on you. Observe their body language, listen to what they are saying to see if it seems like they are lying. If they get overly defensive, or start acting suspicious, then it is a strong indicator they may be cheating on you. But whatever you do, don't go through their phone without their permission.

If you suspect them of texting a certain person, call them out on it and ask them to prove it to you that they aren't. If they have NOTHING to hide, they will give you their phone to show you that your suspicions are wrong. An innocent person will always WANT to prove their innocence to you.

BUT if they don't show you willingly and are being very secretive, then it's a big red flag. That would be a big indicator that they have been up to no good behind your back.

However, I MUST say this... If they have shown you their phone and proven their innocence to you, then you must

NOT ask to see their phone again. This will make you look distrusting and paranoid because you have already been proven wrong and it will ruin your relationship.

If you still think they are cheating though, be very observant of their other behaviours because they may just be very good at hiding their unfaithful actions on their phone. And if your suspicions get proven right in a different way, end the relationship.

Like I said before though, never go through each other's phones without their permission because that can end relationships.

How often you should be talking to your partner on the phone

Something that a lot of people struggle with is when they have been with someone for a long time, the amount they text each other will naturally become less and less.

The honeymoon phase will ease off and it won't be as thrilling to text them all the time, and that's ok because it's very normal. But many people think that this is because their partner is losing interest in them, however this isn't always the case.

Sometimes when someone knows they are going to see you in person a lot more, they don't feel the need to text you all the time. This doesn't mean that they have lost interest in you. It simply means that you are in the next phase on your relationship. For example, you don't see many people who have been happily married for years texting each other 24/7.

I would say it's healthy to simply meet each other's texting wants and needs.

Let's say you are somebody who likes to text and talk about your day a lot over the phone, but your partner is somebody who doesn't want to text much, then you both must compromise and meet in the middle.

Don't text them constantly, or you'll look needy and as if you're not respecting your partner's space. But they can't ignore you either because they need to respect and acknowledge your needs and wants in the relationship.

Listen to each other and be understanding of what the other person wants, and meet in the middle, and you'll both be much happier.

What to do if your partner is more interested in their phone than spending time with you

Welcome to one of the most common relationship problems of the modern age!

There is nothing more frustrating than when you are spending time with someone, and they are on their phone the whole time. It's so rude! This creates a lot of arguments in many relationships because people don't feel wanted and desired, and they feel like their partner is a lot more interested in their phone than they are in spending quality time with their partner.

Both you and your partner should be able to do things together without the phone being a problem. Here are a few examples when the phone should be put away...

When you are on a date together

You're there to spend quality time together and ENJOY the date. Being on the phone during a date makes you partner feel unwanted and undesired. Also, it's so rude!

When you are relaxing at home watching a movie together

There's nothing more annoying than watching a show with someone and they are on their phone and having them asking you a million questions because they have no idea what's going on. It makes you feel like they might as well not even be there.

When you are both out on a nature walk together

Enjoy nature. Enjoy chatting to your partner. Make special memories. The only time the phone should come out is to take pictures of you two together with the beautiful scenery.

Lots of people get addicted to their phones, and that addiction can ruin a lot of relationships because someone always feels ignored and replaced by their partner's phone. Don't let that happen to your relationship. If your partner is addicted to their phone and ignores you for their phone, then you need to handle the situation like this...

Have an honest and open conversation with them about how it makes you feel when they ignore you for their phone. Then compromise a set of rules with them...

For example...

- Agree that during dates to put the phone away and enjoy each other's company by having a conversation with each other and being fully present on the date.

- Agree that when you both come home from work etc, to have a conversation with each other before sitting down to scroll on the phone.

- Agree that an hour an evening, the phone gets put to one side and you both enjoy each other's company (even if it's just watching a movie together).

These are very simple rules, but they will make a world of difference! If your partner cares about your feelings, they will follow these rules.

Don't let a phone ruin a potentially amazing relationship, it would be a real shame. It happens to so many people and it's such an easy thing to correct.

MONEY

At some point during your relationship, you and your partner are going to have discussions about money. Many people handle money in their relationships the wrong way. But in this chapter, I am going to be giving you advice and guidance on how to navigate this area of your relationship. Once you know how to navigate the topic of money in a relationship, you should never have any more arguments about it. Let's get into it...

How to manage money in different scenarios in your relationship

Ok, so there are a few different scenarios that determine how money works in a relationship...

You both have full time jobs and no children together

If you both work full time and don't have any children, then your money is your money. There's no questions about it.

Your partner has NO CONTROL over your money, and you have no control over theirs. You are both free to do as you please. You can of course both be generous with your money to each other, but never demand anything from each other.

Also let's say that all of the bills are paid between you both and you want to buy something for yourself... Your partner has no say at all about what you can spend your money on. If they start trying to control what you can or can't do with your money, then that's abusive and controlling behaviour. If you don't have any bills that you have to pay together, then neither of you has any say of what the other can or can't do with their money.

One of you works and the other person doesn't, and you have no children together

I understand that there are many unfortunate circumstances where somebody may lose their job or doesn't work, however the person who has lost their job or doesn't work can't demand any money from their partner. Their partner can help them out and be as generous as they want to be, but it should never be demanded that they do so.

If you hit hard times, and your partner is a good person, they will always help you out and never see you struggle. But if your partner doesn't help you out when you have lost your job, then it proves to me that they are not somebody who you should be with. It shows a lack of empathy and teamwork from them.

You can tell a lot about someone by the way they react when their partner hits hard times.

HOWEVER, you should only help somebody if they are doing their best to help themselves otherwise it creates an unhealthy pattern of co-dependency when they should be trying to get their own job situation under control.

So, if you have a partner who has lost their job, only help them out if they are helping themselves out, otherwise they will start treating you like their own personal bank account and that's not the type of relationship you want to be in.

One of you works whilst the other person stays home and looks after the children

I've seen many arguments because of this situation when it comes to money, but it is actually very simple to navigate…

A lot of people don't see raising a child as a full-time job, BUT it most definitely is! It's one of the most intense full-time jobs you'll ever have in your life. It never stops! However, a lot of people go to work and think that the other person staying at home has been sat around all day doing nothing, when in reality, going to work is much easier than raising a child.

So, it's simple… If you both live together and have a child and one of you is working and the other person is at home raising the child, then the money must go into one big pot. You MUST both sit down and budget correctly and responsibly and you must stick to it. You must break it down in a way that is fair to you both, like this...

- Firstly, make sure ALL of the bills are paid.

- Secondly, see how much money is left over.

- Thirdly, you must then split the money equally between you both, and that money is yours to do whatever you want with.

This way there are NO arguments to be had. If someone complains about this method, then it simply comes down to greed and not treating your partner fairly. This method shows good teamwork and it's a fair system.

Both of you work and have children together

If you both work and have children together, then you should put all of the money earnt into one big pot. No one person in the relationship has full control over the money. But instead, you must treat it like you are a team.

After all of the bills are paid, split the remaining money in half. Then with your half you can do as you please with it.

As a family unit this is by far the healthiest and fairest way to handle this situation.

My partner is irresponsible with money. What can I do about it?

Ok, so when one of you is irresponsible with money, it can be a nightmare scenario in a relationship. It ultimately comes down to whether you live together or not. There are different rules for this depending on living circumstances. Let's get into it...

If you don't live together

If you don't live together, yet your partner is irresponsible with their money, then there's nothing you can really do about it.

Let's say they accumulate a serious amount of debt, or perhaps they gamble their money away, or they simply spend all their money at once, so they have none left... If this is the case, then you need to do this...

Re-evaluate whether you want to be with someone like this. This is because as the relationship progresses you will both eventually live together and possibly have children together, and if you have a partner who is irresponsible with money, then it's a nightmare scenario for you to be in. You don't want to be with someone who is going to drag you down and make their problems become your problems because they have no self-control. It's not fair on you and it will make you miserable.

So, it's simple... If you don't live with someone and they are irresponsible with money, re-evaluate the relationship and assess whether you want to stay with them long term, because they will make their problems become your problems. I've seen this happen too many times.

If you live together

If one of you is irresponsible with money and you have bills to pay together, then you need to assess if they are the right person for you...

If you are the one always picking up the pieces and paying their share of the bills because they are overspending, gambling, or getting themselves into pointless debt, then you need to leave that relationship.

It shows they don't respect you and see you as some sort of cash machine. It's an abusive behaviour when this happens because they are exploiting you because you love them, and they are taking advantage of you.

I highly suggest giving them ONE warning to change their behaviour and that you'll leave them if they don't. Explain to them why it's wrong and how you feel they are exploiting you.

If they are sincerely sorry and start behaving the correct way, then that's great. But if they carry on being irresponsible with money, then you must leave them. It shows that they care more about material things and their own money over their relationship with you. That's not the type of person you want in your life.

How to pay the bills when you live together and one of you earns significantly more than the other (You don't have children together)

This is a conversation that can cause many arguments...

Firstly, it's simple if you have kids together... All the money earnt goes into one big pot and budgeted properly in a mature way. But if you don't have children together then it needs to be handled a bit differently. But have no worries because it's very easy to do...

Let's make it an easy number to work with, and let's say that all of the bills come to a total of $3000.

For example: One of you earns $10000 a month and the other person earns $5000 a month, then this is how to FAIRLY pay for the bills in the relationship...

Bill total: $3000
The person who earns $10000 pays $2000
The person who earns $5000 pays $1000

This way it works out that 20% of each person's income goes towards the bills. The percentage paid out of each person's income should be EQUAL, and that way it's fair.

This way you are working as a team. And if you keep this structure throughout your entire relationship when paying the bills, then you will have no problems.

When you should and shouldn't get a Prenup

I fully understand why some people want a prenup, and I understand why some people don't want a prenup... So, I will give my opinion on this topic, and I believe this is 100% the correct way to handle the prenup situation...

What's important is how you two met before you decided to get married that makes a big difference to whether you should get a prenup or not.

You met each other when you both had very little money

So, you first met each other when you both had no money, and now you have been together for quite a few years...

Then over time, one of you makes a lot of money, and now you both want to get married...

If this is the case then you should NOT get a prenup because:

- You loved each other when you both had no money.

- You have both proven you are in the relationship for the right reasons.

- You have built your empire together.

- Perhaps without the help of their partner, the other person wouldn't have been as successful.

You started a life together with nothing, now moving forward as a married couple, everything you have built together is yours to share, and I think that's a beautiful thing.

You first met when one of you has a lot of money and the other person doesn't

If this is the case, then this is when you SHOULD get a prenup.

This is protecting the person who has made a lot of money and gained their assets before you have both met.

If the person with no money refuses to get married if they must sign a prenup, then to me, it shows that they don't care about spending their life with the other person. Instead, it shows that they only want to be with the other person if they can have access to their money and assets, and that's not what love and marriage is about.

If you truly love someone you will sign a prenup because

you will be understanding that the other person will want to protect themselves.

Also, because the person who doesn't have the money shows that they aren't marrying them for their money, 99% of the time, the person with the money will be extremely generous because they will feel valued and wanted for who they are, not what they have.

In a relationship you financially support each other during tough times

Money comes, and money goes. Everyone in their lives will have good times and bad times with money. And sometimes when you are in a relationship, one of you may be doing great financially, and the other person may be doing bad. But a good person always supports their partner in times of need.

Let's say your partner loses their job through no fault of their own... They will be feeling very worried and anxious. It's then your responsibility as their partner to offer your love and support. Let them know that you have got their back financially and they don't need to worry about anything, and you will help them as much as you can until they get back on their feet. When you do this, it will strengthen the relationship massively and its exactly how people in healthy relationships behave.

However, only support someone who is trying their best to get back on their feet, otherwise they are exploiting you. They can't sit around the house doing nothing and throwing a pity party for themselves when you pick up all the pieces. They must be proactively trying their best to help themselves. If they are, then give them all the support you can. If you can do this, I promise you that you will be greatly rewarded for your help and loyalty in the future if they are a good person. They will know that when they needed you, you were there for them, and that means a lot! You will have a lot of good karma coming your way...

HOUSEWORK

You've moved in with your partner and then reality hits you! You now have the element of housework in your relationship to think about!

Dividing the housework should actually be one of the simplest things in a relationship, but for many people it's not. The main cause of arguments in a relationship regarding housework is that somebody isn't pulling their weight and is very lazy, whilst the other person does the majority of the work, and it's not fair! There are exceptions to this of course and I will cover them in this chapter...

Here is some very useful guidance on how to manage the housework in your relationship...

How to divide the housework in your relationship

It all comes down to how much either of you works. Remember, you are a team in life, and the housework is no exception to this rule. When one person can't do it, the other person must help out.

I'll break it down into mini sections that are easier to understand...

You both work full-time

This one is simple. You split the housework straight down the middle. 50/50. No questions asked.

If one of you cooks, the other does the washing up.
If you make lunch, they make dinner.
If you clean the kitchen, they clean the bathroom.
They do the laundry, you do the dusting.

It's really that simple.

Come to an agreement on which chores you are both happy doing and stick to that.

If there is a chore both of you really hates doing, then take it in turns doing it.

If you stick to this system, then there is no possible way there can be an argument about the housework. And if there is, it's because the person complaining about it is being lazy and selfish. It means they don't see you as an equal, and that's not someone that you want to be in a relationship with. You are their partner, not their servant.

One of you works more than the other

Let's say that one of you works 40 hours a week, and the other person works 15 hours a week...

If this is the case, then the person who is working less must do more of the housework. It's only fair. I'm not saying that they must do everything, but they should be doing a more.

For example, if you have a day off and your partner is working, then you can't expect them to come home and cook for you whilst you've had the whole day off. That's not fair.

Cook for them, so when they come home, they will have a nice home cooked meal. And of course, if you are working and they aren't, then they must do the same for you.

Once you both have this mentality it will strengthen the relationship because you are both working as a team.

One of you works and the other doesn't

This scenario has a couple of factors to consider. I'll break this bit into little sections...

If they are working and you don't have any big responsibilities in your life, (i.e. you don't have children to look after), then it's your responsibility to do the majority of the housework.

HOWEVER, your partner can't treat you like their servant, and they must tidy up after themselves. For example, they can't simply throw their clothes on the floor and expect you to pick it up for them. They must still behave like an adult and clean up after themselves. But when they are at work and the laundry hasn't been done, then it's your responsibility to do it.

Now, let's say that you do have big responsibilities in your own life, then the rules slightly change...

For example, they work full-time, and you are a full-time parent at home. If this is the case, then the housework becomes 50/50 again. This is because when you have a big responsibility, such as being a full-time parent, it's very tough and it's nearly impossible to do that AND keep on top of the housework, and sometimes being at work is actually easier than being at home. So, again, if this is the case then the housework needs to be divided 50/50.

What to do if your cleaning standards are higher than your partner's

This can be a tricky situation to be in because somebody's version of clean might not be your version of clean. And there's nothing more frustrating than when you are a clean person, and you have to deal with messy and unhygienic people. To navigate this, it needs to be handled correctly to avoid arguments in the relationship. So, this is what I suggest...

Let's say that you are the clean one in the relationship and your partner is the unclean one. First of all, let's talk about hygiene standards...

I personally hate it when people are unhygienic because there's no excuse for it. So, I suggest being very firm with your partner if they are unhygienic and say to them that they MUST become a hygienic person if they want to be in a relationship with you. Health and safety come first; and if they are the type of person to spread germs because of pure laziness, then that is never ok. Again, be firm and say it's non-negotiable.

If they resist you on this, then pull away from them. It's gross and there's no need for it. Don't get sick because of their stupidity.

Now, when it comes to messiness it's a little bit different... Messiness can be frustrating, but it's not going to make you sick. If they are messy and you're overly neat, then you need to meet in the middle. They can't simply throw their clothes on the floor or leave the table in an absolute mess and expect you to tidy it away for them. That's not fair.

Instead, you both need to sit down and have a conversation on how you can compromise so you're both happy with your living conditions... Things that you both can and can't live without when it comes to messiness.

For example, if it drives you crazy when they throw their clothes on the floor, say to them to put it in the washing basket, or in the wardrobe. It takes little effort on their behalf, and it makes you feel much happier and more relaxed.

But, if they do this for you, then you must be a little lenient with them as well. Don't nag them if it's minor things that annoy you because you have a very high standard of neatness. Recognise that they might not see it as important as you do and learn to let some things go.

When you both are considerate of each other, it will make your relationship much more pleasant.

CHEATING

It's an unfortunate thing, but cheating happens so often in many relationships. It is one of the worst things that can happen in a relationship. As soon as someone cheats, the relationship is forever changed, and it is over.

What some people say is cheating, other people might say it's not cheating. Some people are very strict on what they consider cheating, whereas other people are far more lenient.

I'm a firm believer in what the person's intentions are to whether it is considered cheating or not. Someone may say something that in their own mind was purely innocent, whereas their partner may assume that what they have said is cheating, when in reality, it wasn't.

In this chapter we are discuss cheating and how you should navigate it if it happens in your relationship...

What is cheating?

Different people have different views on what is cheating and what isn't cheating. People who are in a monogamous relationship will have completely different boundaries to people who are in an open relationship. But I still think there's universal constants of what is cheating and what isn't cheating in regard to 99% of relationships.

First of all, I believe that INTENTIONS of somebody's actions is the most important factor when passing judgement if something is cheating or not. If someone has bad intentions, then 100% of the time it will be considered cheating.

This is a list of behaviours that I consider cheating...

- Having any form of sexual intercourse with someone outside of your relationship

- Flirting with the intent of taking things further

- Flirting by making sexual comments to someone outside of your relationship

- Meeting up with people who have displayed sexual interest towards you without your partner knowing

- Having an active online dating profile

- Making sexually inappropriate comments to someone outside of your relationship

- Inappropriate physical touching of someone outside of your relationship

- Following random people's social medias that exclusively exist to make sexual content (If your partner has expressed that they don't like it)

- Liking, commenting, sharing, saving (any engagement) on other people's social media posts that are exclusively sexual content, or 'Thirst Traps' (Content that is made to attract sexual attention from the audience) (If your partner has expressed that they don't like it)

- Purposely hiding from your partner who you are talking to because you have sexual feelings towards that person

I understand that if people are in an open relationship that not all of these are considered cheating. However, ALL of these are considered cheating in monogamous relationships.

Why you shouldn't cheat

Honestly, there is no excuse for cheating. I don't care how bad a relationship is, just leave if you feel like you may end up cheating. There's no need to cheat.

If you do cheat, then you will be forever branded as a 'cheater'. That's a mark against your name that doesn't go away.

Many people ask before getting into a relationship with you, 'Have you ever cheated?', and if the answer is 'yes' then it will seriously put them off the idea of dating you, and understandably they may not continue to date you.

On the other hand, if someone asks you if you have cheated before and you say 'no', then it makes you more attractive and they won't be nervous about getting into a relationship with you.

Many people believe 'Once a cheat, always a cheat', and they aren't going to get into a relationship with you if they believe there is a chance they will get cheated on.

Don't cheat. It's never worth it. If you're in a bad relationship, or if you like someone else, then leave your relationship and date other people.

Why people cheat

There are many reasons why people cheat. Sometimes it's because of their upbringing, another reason could be social conditioning, other times it could be due to their past relationships.

In this section I'm going to explain to you some of the reasons why people cheat...

Their parents cheated on each other

If someone has been raised in a household where one of their parents cheated on the other, then it will significantly increase the chances of that person cheating. This is because they have been raised to think that cheating is normal and acceptable behaviour because their parents are their earliest role models.

If the parent who got cheated on always forgives the cheater, their child will then grow up to become an adult that thinks that every time they cheat their partner will take them back and forgive them. This is because that's what they have seen their parents do.

But if their partner doesn't take them back, they think that their partner is weird and unforgiving, even though they are the one in the wrong for cheating.

Of course, not everyone who has parents who cheat on each other will end up cheaters themselves. But it does increase the likelihood of them being a person who thinks cheating is normal.

However, if someone grows up with parents who cheat, and they witness how destructive it can be, they could go the totally opposite way and become a person who would never cheat because they don't want to repeat the same process in their own relationships.

So, it does depend on how they view their parents who cheated on each other, and if they see them as negative influences or role models to emulate.

Their partner cheated on them in a previous relationship, and they are repeating the process to resolve it within their own mind. (This is their subconscious driving them to do this)

If someone experiences very strong emotions through events that causes emotional trauma (which cheating can often do), their brain will sometimes try and process their emotions in 1 of 3 ways...

1. They repeat the thing that gave them trauma. (In this case, cheat on their own partner for their brain to make sense of being cheated on themselves)

2. Avoid the thing that gave them trauma. (They would never cheat or be with someone who has cheated)

3. They help others who are going through a similar trauma that they have experienced themselves. (A way for them to make sense of it through somebody else's experiences)

Once you understand that this is how some people's minds cope with unprocessed trauma, you can then start to understand why someone may cheat when they have been cheated on before.

It's still no excuse to cheat on someone, and you should still leave them for cheating on you. It's their problem, not yours. And it's not fair for them to make it your problem.

Social conditioning has taught them that it's normal to cheat

I hate this as it's such a stupid reason to cheat on someone, but it's a very common reason. So, what I mean by social conditioning influencing people to cheat is this...

These days in the media, the media hyper fixates on cheating whether it be through reality TV, dramas, gossip columns etc. This is because it is scandalous and interesting for people to watch. If this is always in front of viewers eyes, they will start to think that everyone cheats, and that cheating is a normal behaviour. Also, many of their friends will think the same way. This creates a giant domino effect within their social circle...

When people are talking to their friends about cheating on their partner, and lots of their friends are exposed to the same media and influences, instead of correcting their friend's way of thinking and convincing them that cheating is wrong, they will laugh about it and assume it's normal because of what they have been exposed to themselves. Thus, creating a friendship group where everyone thinks it's normal to cheat. This way of thinking is spreading because it's more prominent in many different aspects of modern culture, and it's very sad to see.

It's hard to convince someone that cheating isn't a normal acceptable behaviour when they have been socially conditioned their whole lives to think it is normal to cheat.

They've lost attraction for their partner, but they don't want to leave their partner because they don't want to hurt their feelings

This is a very common reason for people to cheat. They lose attraction for their partner, so they start a sexual relationship with someone else to fill the void they feel in their own relationship that their current partner isn't fulfilling.

The reason they do this behind their partner's back is because they are in conflict with themselves. They know cheating is wrong, but they also want to spare their partner's feelings because they do like their partner as a person but just aren't sexually attracted to them anymore. So instead of telling them the truth, they think they are doing them a kindness by keeping it a secret. But as many of us know, the truth will always come to light. And keeping it a secret is not a kindness.

If someone does this, they are living a false life, and forcing a false life upon their partner. Their partner might think everything is great, but the whole time they are getting cheated on behind their back. Imagine if they found out they've been cheated on 5 years later after staying with that person all that time... They would feel like they've wasted 5 years of their life. That's not fair on them at all.

If someone loses sexual attraction for their partner, and they've done everything they can to rekindle the attraction, but it's still not there, they should end the relationship before they start to think about cheating on their partner. It's the right thing to do.

They don't respect their partner

People with this type of personality must be avoided at all costs when dating and in relationships. They are nothing but trouble.

Some people will cheat on their partner because they feel superior to them and don't respect them as a person. A lot of the time this person doesn't respect anybody and is a very selfish person. They will only get into a relationship with someone who they can treat like this because it makes them feel superior. They wouldn't get into a relationship with someone who has very firm boundaries who would leave them if they got cheated on.

If you feel like this is your partner, leave the relationship.

What to do if someone has cheated on you

I'm going to make this as blunt as it needs to be... If someone has cheated on you, then don't try to repair that relationship. Leave them and don't ever look back.

If your partner cheated on you, it is one of the most disrespectful things that they can do to you in a relationship. 99% of the time they will do it again, even if they promised you that they won't.

I rarely see a case where a cheater won't cheat again sometime in the future. It may take them a week to cheat again, it may take them 10 years, but most of the time they will cheat again. Don't let yourself be someone who allows people to disrespect them to this calibre, and don't allow them to continue being in your life.

If they cheat on you, they don't love you. Some people may argue with me on that, but I am 100% correct. If someone truly loves you, they wouldn't ever want to hurt you.

If you stay in a relationship where someone has cheated on you, that relationship will always be ruined in my opinion. It will never be the fairy-tale relationship that you want it to be, and that you deserve. It will always be stained by the cheater's actions.

So, again... If someone cheats on you or has ever cheated on you (even if it was a long time ago), leave them and don't look back. They don't deserve to be in your life. You deserve someone who loves you and treats you the way you deserve to be treated.

I also want to add that if someone cheats on you, it has NOTHING to do with you. I don't want you to feel like there is something wrong with you, because there isn't.

You see some of the most amazing people get cheated on, and it's not because they did anything wrong, it's because their partner wasn't a good person. A cheater will always cheat regardless of how amazing you are. Also, if they were a good person, they would simply leave the relationship instead of cheating if the relationship is going badly.

So, again, I promise you that if you got cheated on, it's not your fault. The person who did the cheating is the person with something wrong with them.

JEALOUSY IN RELATIONSHIPS

Jealousy is something that can destroy a relationship if not addressed and kept under control. I have seen many couples break up over jealousy and it's such a shame to see, especially if it was something that should have never been an issue in the first place.

Sometimes people get jealous of their partner's past. Sometimes of what is presently happening. Sometimes of future events that someone will think their partner MIGHT end up doing. Either way, in this chapter I will be addressing jealousy and how to overcome it...

Jealousy over your partner's past

There are many different scenarios where people feel jealous of their partner's past. Perhaps they are jealous of the relationship their partner had with an ex. Maybe they feel jealous of their partner's sexual history. They might even be jealous or territorial about people who their partner has only previously been on dates with. Either way, none of this jealousy is productive to anyone in the relationship. So, firstly let's talk about feeling jealous of your partner's sexual history...

Jealousy over your partner's sexual history

Ok, I get it... Thinking about your partner's previous sex life is a disgusting thought to many of us. The thought of them being intimate with someone else is simply something that we never want to think of. Yet many of us (even against our better judgement) succumb to curiosity and ask our partner questions about their previous sex life. The only outcome you can get from doing this is going to be a negative outcome.

Let's say your partner opens up and tells you about their previous sex life, and you find out they had a very 'adventurous' sex life with their ex... The only thing that's going to happen is that you compare it to the sex life that you now share with your partner. Perhaps what they told you was something you haven't done together yet. It's going to make you feel jealous and can cause unnecessary problems in your relationship.

When it comes to your partner's previous sex life, you have 2 options:

Option 1: Ask them about it and make yourself feel grossed out and jealous.

Option 2: Never ask them and save yourself the trouble of finding out something you wish you never knew.

In my opinion you should take option 2. Sometimes

not knowing is the best option. In this scenario, what you don't know can't hurt you. And if you love your partner, then leave the past in the past otherwise you'll just gross yourself out. Some things just don't need to be spoken about...

Being jealous about your partner's previous relationships and the experiences they shared with an ex

Perhaps you and your partner have spoken about what it was like in your previous relationships and the experiences that you shared with your exes, and I'm not just talking about sexual experiences either. I'm referring to things such as holidays they have been on, or different date experiences that they haven't yet shared with you. This can gross you out and make you feel jealous, and sometimes a little insecure because you may be wondering why you haven't had these experiences with your partner yet.

If this is the case, I want to you know this... Your relationship and your partner's previous relationships are NOT the same and shouldn't be treated as such.

I want you to view it from this perspective... Your love journey is a like a book. Each book has different chapters. Within each chapter you will have different events happen. Sometimes there are new characters, sometimes characters leave the story and sometimes there are characters who are forever present in the story. Either way, before your partner met you, they were going through an entirely different chapter of their story; one where they haven't met you yet. BUT now that they have met you, they have started a new chapter in their love story with you. Hopefully a much better chapter with more exciting experiences. Also, the book isn't finished yet and you both have a long way to go and there will be new chapters that you both share together.

Once you look back, you'll realise that it wasn't worth being jealous of their previous relationships because they can't compare to the experiences you have and will both share together.

Feeling jealous of what is presently happening with your partner

Ok, so a situation that makes a lot of people feel jealous and territorial is when their partner is getting sexual/flirtatious attention from other people. This can cause many arguments within the relationship. However, I want you to start thinking about it like this...

1. Is your partner seeking sexual/flirtatious attention from others?

If they are seeking sexual/flirtatious attention from other people, then you are effectively being made to feel jealous and it's very disrespectful to you and your relationship if they do this.

If this is the case in your relationship, you need to leave the relationship because I view this as a form of them cheating.

2. They are not inviting this type of attention from people, and it is given freely to them without them doing anything...

If this is making you overly jealous, you need to look within yourself and understand that your jealousy is coming from an insecurity of yours and it's not your partner's fault.

Address the root cause of your jealousy to overcome this. For example, did your previous partner cheat on you? And because of your past relationship, does it trigger feelings of jealousy when other people try to flirt with your current partner?

Be honest with yourself as it will take a lot of self-reflection. Don't let your past ruin your future.

3. If your partner isn't cheating on you or gaslighting you into feeling jealous, but instead, is a loving kind person to you that many people just so happen to find attractive, I want you to know this...

Your partner is going home with you. They are sharing experiences with you. They are getting into bed at night with you. They are building a future with you. NOBODY ELSE. You win!

Please do not let something like jealousy ruin that for you. I've seen jealousy break up many good relationships. Don't let that happen to you.

WHEN TO REACH RELATIONSHIP MILESTONES

As a dating and relationship expert I'm always being asked about how long certain milestones should take to reach in a relationship. It can be confusing for many people because some people's relationships move very quickly, and they live happily ever after. Sometimes couples move quickly, and it all falls apart. On the other hand, some people take their time reaching relationship milestones and it doesn't work out. But some couples take their time, and everything goes great for them.

Everyone is different and moves at different paces in life. Love is not a race, it's an experience.

HOWEVER, you shouldn't rely on the fact that things are always going to go smoothly for you like they do for other very lucky people. You need to make smart decisions before reaching some milestones in your relationship, otherwise you can end up in some terrible situations.

In this section I will be giving you advice to help guide you to make the right decisions, so you don't rush things, so your life becomes much easier...

How long it should take to make it 'official'

I get asked this question A LOT... Lots of people end up dating someone for 6 months, sometimes more, and never make it an official relationship with the person they are dating. This is a HUGE mistake! If your relationship isn't clearly defined that you two are officially in a relationship together, then I guarantee 99% of the time, that someone's feelings will end up getting hurt.

I've seen many people THINK that they are in a relationship with someone because 6 months has passed. Then the person they are dating drops the bombshell that they aren't in a relationship with them and are 'keeping their options open'. Then the person who thought they were in a relationship becomes very upset and very untrusting of other people in the future because they feel like they have been betrayed.

Many people will string other people along and not make it 'official' with them because they like keeping their options open and having someone else there as a backup and for entertainment purposes. It's very sad to see and morally very wrong.

I want you to think about it like this... If you've been dating someone for 3 months, which is around 90 days, and that person isn't sure if they want to be in a relationship with you or not, then I want you to stop dating that person.

90-100 days is a very long time to know if you want to

be with someone or not. And if they can't make their mind up in 3 months, then I promise you, they aren't the one for you.

As a bonus, here's 3 things you can say to someone you are dating to find out how they view you in relation to them...

1. Say to them...

'Other people have asked me for a date. I don't want to date other people though as I'm enjoying only dating you. Do you feel the same way?'

If they say 'yes', then say this...

'Well, I don't want to date anybody else, and you don't want to date anybody else, so shall we just go exclusive?'

2. Say to them...

'I have a question... When we are in a social situation together, how would you like me to introduce you in relation to me?'

3. Say to them...

'My friend asked if me and you are together. I didn't know what to tell them though because me and you haven't spoken about it yet. It would be good to know what you think in case I do get asked again in the future.'

All 3 of these things to say will be very helpful in finding out how the other person thinks of you.

When you should move in together

Moving in together is one of the biggest steps you can take in your relationship. You will truly get to know your partner, sometimes for better, sometimes for worse. Either way, it is a necessary step to further progress your relationship.

I expect you have heard stories of people who moved in together straight away and lived happily ever after. I also expect you've heard many stories of people who have been happily together for years, then moved into together after a long time, and then broke up because they aren't right for each other.

In my opinion, I believe there's only one way of doing it to ensure you are both right for each other before fully committing to living together. I recommend moving in together gradually...

For example, start off by staying overnight at theirs (or yours) a few nights a week, and then eventually start staying over more frequently.

I recommend doing it like this because a lot of people can't handle a big sudden change to their home environment. But if you slowly start living together you will learn each other's habits and behaviours and can discuss them if they are an issue before fully committing to moving in together. So, by the time you live together any of the potential problems you could have faced would have already been resolved.

If I had to give a timeline of when you should start living together (or beginning the process) I would say to do it after being together for 6 months. This way it's not too fast, but it's also not too slow.

You don't want to be with someone for 5 years then find out you can't live together. That would be terribly frustrating. However, like I said, this is just my recommendation because you could start living together after knowing each other for only a month and live happily ever after! (It does happen)

You will never know if you are truly compatible until you live together.

How long to wait until you buy a house together

Buying a house with someone is one of the biggest decisions you will ever make in your life. It's a HUGE financial tie to someone, comes with a lot of stress if you are buying a house with the wrong person, and can cause some serious arguments and lead to the relationship ending. But if you buy a house with the right person, you can have a beautiful home together full of love.

You MUST be sure you are buying a house with the right person... Here's my recommendations to think about before you buy a house with your partner...

1. Your age and your partner's age...

If you are going to buy a house with your partner, I HIGHLY recommend that you wait until you are both at least 30 years old. This is because, for example, if you are both 25, by the time you get to 30 years old you will be very different people. And if they end up being a person who you don't want to be with, then you will have a huge financial tie to this person, and that is a terrible position to be in.

But if you wait until you're both at least 30 years old, then you will have more life experience and be much wiser on how to handle many different situations, including who you make financial ties with.

I have had many people tell me that they wish they never bought a house with an ex when they were younger because it became one of the worst decisions of their lives.

If you two want to be together forever, then waiting for a bit before you buy a house shouldn't be an issue.

2. Rent together before you buy!

Before you live together, you need to see how responsible your partner is with paying their bills, cleaning, maintaining the home etc. If they are great at all of these things, then you know it's a safer move to buy a house with this person, because at least you'll know you won't have to act like a parent to them.

On the other hand, if they can't do any of these things responsibly, then you know buying a house with them would be the wrong move and it would bring a lot of stress to your life.

So, rent together before you buy so you know what you're getting yourself into!

3. Get married before you buy a house OR at least be together for a minimum of 3 years...

Ok, I understand that not everyone wants to get married and that's ok, however I've had many people tell me that they felt buying a house with someone and then breaking up with them was a lot more stressful than ending a marriage.

This is because when money and property get involved when two people end a relationship, you start to see a far more sinister side to people. Money does weird things to people, so you must protect yourself.

I HIGHLY recommend being together for at least 3 years before buying a house together. In that time, you should have rented and lived together, been through ups and downs, and shared responsibilities with each other.

BEFORE you purchase a house together, be sure to have a VERY strong relationship where you want to be together forever...

How long to wait until you get married

Getting married is a very big decision and it will affect your life in many ways. Similar to buying a house, marriage will tie you to that person for a very long time even when things don't work out. Because of this you want to make sure you are entering a marriage with the right person. So here are a few basic rules to follow when you are thinking about getting married...

1. Wait until you are at least 30 years old...

Some people marry in their early 20's and it works out for them, but it doesn't happen very often. This is because people change as they grow. The person you are in your 20's will not be the person you are in your 30's, and the same will be said about your partner.

If you are marrying in your early 20's, be aware that the person you marry now will be very different when they are 30. And if they end up being the type of person you don't want to be with, then you will be looking to divorce them, and this is a very stressful and tough process for a lot of people to go through.

I've spoken to many people who said they wished they never got married in their early 20's, and wished they waited until they were at least 30 years old. If you think you will both be together forever then waiting until you're 30 years old is no big deal, correct?

2. Get to know everything you can about that person before you marry them...

You need to know their money habits, their living standards, how they communicate, you need to see them at their best and worst to know if they are the right person for you. And on the flip side, they need to know all of this about you.

Many people get married and then end up getting some nasty surprises they never saw coming because they rushed into a marriage. Don't let that be you. So, take your time and get to know EXACTLY who you're marrying in every way.

3. Be together for 3 years before you get married even if you are over 30 years old...

If you want to be with them forever, what's the rush? After 3 years of being with someone, you should know enough about them to make a good decision if they are the right person for you before making a lifelong commitment.

Do all these things before getting married and you'll have a far better idea if marriage is the right move for you and your partner.

How long to wait until you have children together

Who you have children with is without a doubt the most important decision of your life. If you have children with the right person, you will have a much easier life and your children will have a wonderful parent, which is exactly what anyone in their right mind would want when having children with someone. But if you have children with the wrong person, it can seriously ruin many aspects of your life, give you an extreme amount of stress, and your children will have a terrible parent, which is very upsetting. So, when choosing to have children with someone, you need to be VERY selective about who you choose.

This is just my opinion, but this is backed up by MANY different people who also agree with me...

If you can, wait until at least your late 20s to have children. There are so many advantages to having children the older you become. Having children when you are younger is much more difficult. But the longer you wait to have children, the more advantages there are.

This is why having children when you are in your early 20s is much more difficult:

1. You won't be as financially stable. (Usually)

2. You wouldn't have had enough life experiences to make informed decisions as much as you would have if you waited until you were older.

3. You will view the world very differently when you are older.

4. Having children when you are younger may impact your career. If you wait until you are older to have children, you will have a better chance at building a good career. (This isn't the case for everyone, but it does impact a lot of people this way)

5. When you are a young adult, planting your roots in life can be very stressful (such as moving out, starting a new career etc). But it's made 10 times harder when you need to look after a child at the same time because their needs come before yours.

These are important factors to consider when raising children.

For example, if you decide to have children in your early 20s, who you choose to have children with will be very different to your choices at age 30, 99% of the time. So, just wait until you are at least in your late 20s to have children. I have met so many people who said that they wished they waited until they were older to have children because they ended up having children with the wrong person.

Now, onto how long a sensible amount of time is to have been in a relationship with someone until you have children with them...

Be with them for at least 3 years before having children

with them. Exactly for the same reasons as buying a house and marriage. You need to get to know them in every way before making a lifelong decision that ties you to them.

Having children with someone is an even bigger commitment than buying a house or getting married because you can sell a house, get divorced, and eventually have no ties with that person. However, if you have children with someone, you have ties to that person for life.

I've met many people who wish they took their time getting to know someone a lot longer before having children with them, because if they knew what they knew about that person now, they never would have had children with them in the first place.

When choosing who to have children with, don't let impulsive decisions and emotions override logical thinking. You must be deeply in love with your partner, and they must prove they are a great partner to you, and prove they have the qualities that will make them a great parent to your children.

DON'T RUSH THE MOST IMPORTANT DECSION OF YOUR LIFE!

WORDS OF WISDOM FROM A RELATIONSHIP EXPERT

In this chapter I'm going to be giving you some words of wisdom that you can apply to your own relationship. Every relationship is different, but there are pieces of advice that apply to EVERYONE's relationships.

Also, there are words of wisdom in this chapter that apply directly to YOU. Perhaps the words of wisdom in this chapter will alter the way you think about relationships entirely. I know for me that they have changed the way that I think.

I hope you enjoy this chapter, and it gives you a new perspective for yourself and your relationship...

Ask yourself, 'What do I bring to the relationship?'

This is a fascinating question for you and your partner to ask yourselves. Quite often, when I ask someone this question, I will get a better understanding of whether someone truly knows what it means to be in a relationship or not.

So, I want you and your partner to write down or say to each other 10 things that you bring to the relationship.

Listen to their answers and it will tell you a lot about the way they view your relationship...

Now, this is the secret to why I ask this question... For 9/10 of those answers you give, you can say whatever you like. Perhaps you say that you are attractive, or you're an amazing conversationalist, or you are funny etc. All of this is great, however it's not the main answer I am looking for...

Most people answer this question by saying things about themselves. And I understand why people do this because the question is directed that way. However, if someone understands the true meaning of what it is to be in a relationship, they will say things that directly apply to their partner.

So, the one answer I'm actually looking for is (or a variation of) ... 'I will love and support my partner.' This is very interesting as not many people give this answer, but they should...

People get excited by this question because it gives them the opportunity to highlight their best qualities. But when someone makes a good partner, they are thinking more about their partner than themselves. Because of this, they will give an answer that relates to their partner.

Give it a go and ask people what they bring to a relationship. The results are very interesting...

Do you need distractions from your relationship to be happy?

Ok, so a lot of people broke up with their partner during the covid lockdowns. People stayed in their houses with their partner for most of the day, sometimes even 24 hours a day, for a long period of time. And this time with only each other for company, and away from the outside world, exposed A LOT of problems in many people's relationships. It showed them that they don't actually like each other as much as they thought they did.

Before the lockdowns, people had real-world distractions of going to work, going to see their friends and family, doing their hobbies etc, and this gave them an escape from their relationship. But then all of those distractions got taken away and they had to be with their partner without an easy way of escaping the relationship in day-to-day life. This resulted in many couples breaking up because they weren't right for each other.

So, a big indication to whether a couple is right for each other comes down to a simple question... 'Would you be happy in your relationship if there were no distractions from the outside world?'

If you both answer 'yes', to me it shows that you are good for each other because you don't need external sources of entertainment or escapes to avoid your relationship.

Instead, your relationship is your escape from the world...

It's something to think about. I have always been proven right to whether people are in the right relationship by the way they answer this simple question...

Prevention is better than the cure

This is another quote that my dad used to say to me growing up, 'Prevention is better than the cure'. This is 100% true! I have lived many aspects of my life to this quote and I'm very thankful that I did.

Many people get themselves into bad situations in relationships because they forget to do the little things to maintain their relationship. Then the outcome of this is the relationship turns bad and then both people need to fix the situation. But if they just did the simple little things that make a relationship work in the first place, then there would be nothing to fix.

Don't wait until the relationship is in a real bad place to start working on things. You should make it a habit to be always working on the relationship. Little and often care to the relationship, even when everything is going great, will go a long way!

SPEAK UP!

Many people don't get what they want in their relationship, or they don't feel like their needs are being met, because they don't speak up about it. Many people simply expect their partner to know what they want, and a lot of the time, people are very unaware of what their partner's wants and needs are.

Not speaking up about what you want or need comes from a lot of people's upbringings. Many of us are taught from a young age not to speak up and vocalise what we want because it will cause 'hassle' for others.

In some instances, being quiet is the right thing to do, but most of the time you MUST speak up and ask for what you want! If you aren't happy in a situation, then it will start to affect those around you because of your mannerisms and this can cause a lot of friction between people. Whereas if you said what you wanted from the start, it would prevent a lot of arguments.

A lot of people in relationships will stay quiet for a long time to keep the peace, but this can build resentment and will feel like a pressure cooker about to go off. Then one day someone in the relationship does something wrong and then EVERYTHING comes out and massive arguments take place, and then one person is left utterly confused.

This ends a lot of relationships because instead of your wants and needs being addressed straight away, you have let these negative emotions build up into something massive over time.

So, I will keep it simple... If you want something, ask for it. People aren't mind readers. Do this from the start and you will avoid a lot of problems further down the line.

Are they your peace or are they your storm?

This is a simple way of telling if your relationship is a healthy one or a toxic one... When you think of your partner, do you see them as your PEACE or your STORM?

- Are you calm around them?

- Are they calm around you?

- Do they make you feel safe?

- Do you get excited to see them?

- Does your relationship feel like an escape from the rest of the world for you?

If the answer is 'yes' to these questions, that's fantastic because that's how your relationship should feel.

Now, on the other hand...

- Does your relationship feel chaotic?

- Do they stress you out?

- Do they make you feel bad about yourself?

- Are you always arguing with each other?

- Does seeing them feel like a chore to you?

If the answer is 'yes' to these questions, then your relationship isn't a healthy one and needs a lot of work, or the relationship needs to be ended.

'Are they your peace or are they your storm?' is a simple question to answer but reveals so much about your relationship. It's definitely something to think about...

Your relationship doesn't define who you are. You must have your own identity

Whether the relationship is going good or bad, lots of people make their relationship their identity and lose who they were before the relationship. I understand it can be easy to see your relationship as a big part of your identity, and to some extent there is truth in that (I will explain more of this in the next section), but at the same time you MUST have your own life and identity separate from your relationship.

Lots of people in relationships neglect their life outside of the relationship, such as:

- Forgetting about seeing friends as much

- Not doing their hobbies

- Feeling that they must spend ALL their time with their partner.

These things are not healthy for yourself or your relationship. In fact, it's a slippery slope that can eventually lead to the end of a relationship. This is because all the things that you did as an individual is what made you attractive to your partner in the first place.

Have you ever known somebody who was an amazing character and then got into a relationship, and then lost that spark of who they are because they are so obsessed with their relationship and never talk about anything else?...

Well, I'm sure you have, as we all know someone like that. But when their relationship ends, (which a lot of the time when it's like this, it does end), they are completely lost as an individual and have no idea what to do with their lives. Well, don't become like this person because you will be miserable and will have to rebuild your identity from scratch because you neglected all the things that made you who you are.

Also, your partner will lose attraction for you if you don't retain your own identity. They fell for you because of who you are as a person. If you completely change, then you won't be the person that they fell for. Then this will cause problems in the relationship.

So, keep doing the things that make you who you are and live your own life outside of your relationship, and you and your partner will be much happier.

You and your partner represent each other

Of course, we are all individuals, but when we are in a relationship, we do represent our partner by the way that we behave to some extent.

For example, I want you to think of this scenario...

You and your partner go to a social gathering or a party, and then you need to go somewhere, and your partner is left alone to talk to your friends, family, work colleges etc...

You need to have the upmost faith in your partner that they give a good representation of themselves because if they end up making themselves look like an idiot, it will also make you look like an idiot. This is because people like to judge and gossip about others, and the topic will be about how embarrassing your partner was. It will make you look bad, and it can be quite damaging for your social life.

On the other hand, if your partner is left alone with your friends, family or work colleges and they are charming, polite, and sociable, it will elevate your social value. This is because if your partner comes across very well, it shows you associate yourself with high value people.

Like it or not, we do judge other people on who they choose as a partner, and it can either make you look better or worse depending on how your partner behaves.

If you are in a social situation with your partner, I think that it's a great opportunity to assess how much they value your personal relationship with others...

Very selfish partners won't socially calibrate the situation and act accordingly to represent their partners in a good way. They won't care if people judge you or think you have a terrible choice in a partner because they are too self-absorbed and don't think about their partner's feelings.

But if your partner makes as much effort as they can to represent you in a positive way by being charming, likeable, polite, and sociable, that's a fantastic sign. Even if they end up not forming great connections with people, that's ok, as long as they are trying their best. Trying their best is all that matters, and you should be very happy that they are doing that for you. It shows they respect you and your relationships with others. To be fair, most people will see that your partner is making an effort, and they will love that and only have positive things to say about them, which in turn represents you and your relationship very well.

Does your partner represent you well?

You grow together or you grow apart

This statement is so true.

Some couples start off being a great match, but as life goes on, if one of them continues to grow, whilst the other person is lazy and doesn't grow as a person, they will eventually break up.

Let's say that you work a lot on yourself... You study, exercise, be as social as time allows, ambitious with work, learning new things about yourself and the world around you etc, but your partner doesn't do any of these things and is content on being the same person they were 5 years ago...

Well, what are you 2 going to have in common? NOTHING! What is there for you both to talk about if they are always doing the same thing and not learning anything new?

You both MUST be investing your energies into developing yourselves for the relationship to grow and evolve into the something even better than before.

Once you both do this, you will both be much happier in the relationship because you won't get bored of each other. Also, it's very attractive when you see your partner working on themselves because it shows desirable traits within their personality.

If they want to make you a priority, they will!

It's a terrible feeling when you don't feel like a priority to your partner. For example, when you want to spend some quality time together, but they always have an excuse as to why they can't. Or sometimes they don't even try making an excuse, they just don't bother spending time with you.

A big excuse a lot of people make is that they can't spend time with you because they are working a lot...

I hate this excuse. There are many people in extremely demanding jobs who make time for their partner. People ALWAYS MAKE TIME for those who they WANT to make time for. The reason they don't make time is because they can't be bothered to make time. Simple.

Also, another big argument people have is that one of the people in the relationship sees their friends far more than they see their partner...

It's fantastic that they see their friends and I actively encourage it, but there needs to be a balance between the amount of time you see your partner and your friends. If you only just see your partner and neglect seeing your friends, then you will end up losing those friends. But if you only see your friends and never make time for your partner, you will lose your partner. Both partners and friends need your quality time, and if you have a good balance in your social life then both sides will benefit greatly.

So, if your partner doesn't make you feel like a priority then you both need to sit down and have a conversation about it. Explain to them exactly how they make you feel when they don't make you a priority. Ask them why they don't want to spend time with you as there may be a deeper reason that you may not have seen coming.

If they fully listen to you and care about your feelings, then they will actively make an effort and show you that you are a priority in their life.

BUT if they continue not making you a priority, even after they have heard how it makes you feel, then I believe that you should seriously think about leaving that relationship. If they have heard that you are upset, and they don't take actions to correct their behaviour, it shows they don't care about you very much. That's NOT the type of person you want to be in a relationship with.

If they aren't with you at your lowest moments, they don't deserve to be with you at your best moments

Lots of people will love you when you're doing good in life, but not many people will love you when you're at your lowest.

ALL of the best couples I have seen stay with each other during the hardest times. When you reach rock bottom, you find out who truly loves you. And unfortunately, a lot of couples break up when one of the people in the relationship hit hard times in their life. Effectively their partner's love was conditional and on the basis that they will be with them if it is convenient to do so. This isn't the meaning of true love. True love is when you stay together during the best AND the worst of times.

If you are going through something very challenging in your life right now and your partner isn't behaving in a support way, I want you to do this...

Explain to them EXACTLY what you are going through, how it makes you feel, and EXACTLY what you need from them. Make your explanation as clear and simple as possible for them to understand. They may have simply been unaware of the severity of the situation you are in, or they didn't know the correct way to handle it. If that is the case then give them 1 chance to correct their mistakes, as this can be a completely honest mistake of theirs.

However, if you have clearly explained all of these things to your partner and they still don't behave in the correct way, then you need to reassess your entire relationship.

I honestly believe that if your partner wasn't as supportive as they could be when you hit rock bottom, then leave them. They are never going to make an amazing lifelong partner for you, and they will never give you the perfect relationship that you deserve. They are only there when it's convenient for them, and that's not the type of person you want to be with.

Tough times reveal people's true natures. Throughout your whole life you will go through battles, and do you want someone who helps bring you peace during these tough times, or do you want someone who is going to make them harder?

But, on the other hand, if your partner has stuck with you when you have been at your lowest, then cherish that person and don't forget how amazing they were to you. Those are the types of people are rare and deserve your love.

Your partner needs to know you won't stay with them if they don't treat you right

One of the biggest mistakes people make in their love lives is that they stay with someone who doesn't treat them right, in hopes that they will change...

For example, if their partner cheated on them, they think that working through it and coming out the other side together will strengthen the relationship. Or perhaps someone is controlling, and they think that if they make adjustments and compromise with their controlling partner then everything will be easier... Some things you don't have to work through. Leaving them is the only correct option.

A lot of the time, if someone thinks that you're the type of person who is willing to work through anything in a relationship, they will start thinking they can get away with anything. Basically, they will do you wrong now and ask for forgiveness later because they know they will be forgiven. This is a BIG mistake, not only in relationships, but in life.

Your partner needs to have the upmost respect for you and KNOW that you will leave them if they don't treat you the correct way. Of course, there are things you can work through that could be simple misunderstandings, but there are other things that your partner must know that you would leave them for instantly if they even dared to do those things to you.

When you both have this mentality of having the upmost respect for your each other, you both won't make big mistakes and the relationship will be built upon healthy respect for each other. You will both know that if you majorly mess up, you will be single no matter what.

Every couple I know that has this mentality have healthy relationships. It may sound like a very firm approach, but it is a necessary one.

Don't let your past ruin your future

It's a very common occurrence that people allow their past relationships to ruin the relationship they are currently in; and this isn't always their fault, it's simply a product from the unfortunate events that happened in their previous relationships.

For example, if someone has been cheated on, they will naturally be much more suspicious and worried about their current partner's behaviour and may act in unhealthy ways towards their new partner, even if their partner has done nothing wrong.

This can cause problems in a relationship that could have been perfect, but the past relationship has ruined the new relationship for both people, and it's a real shame to see as it's no-one's fault apart from the person who did the cheating in the previous relationship.

Another example is if people's previous partners had a serious lack of communication skills during disagreements and became aggressive. This can cause the other person to become more hostile, or defensive, or even disassociate whenever a disagreement comes up in their new relationship. This is because that's what they felt like they had to do in order to defend themselves from their previous partner. Again, this is a learnt behaviour from being in their previous relationship, and it can make their new partner have serious doubts about the relationship they are now in.

So, I believe it's good to take the time to assess yourself and see if there are any unresolved issues within yourself from a previous relationship...

Be critical of yourself and think, 'Will any of my behaviours stop me from being in a happy, healthy relationship?' If the answer is 'yes', then you need to take time to heal and work on yourself, so you don't let your past ruin your future.

If you can work on yourself and overcome any past relationship issues, and not bring them into your new relationship, then I guarantee that you and your new partner will be much happier. This is because you have used your past as a lesson, and you will use these lessons to help build the amazing relationship that you deserve.

EPILOGUE

It's been my honour and privilege to have shared my knowledge with you about how to achieve the best relationship that you can have. Whether it's with your current partner, or with a future partner, know that you deserve to be happy in your relationship.

Something to keep in mind is that everyone is an individual and has their own unique perspectives on the world, and this needs to be understood when in a relationship with someone. However, there are universal truths that apply to all relationships. For example, showing kindness, consideration and respect for your partner is always a MUST in a relationship for everyone.

One of the most important things in a relationship, that many people forget, is that you must show YOURSELF kindness, consideration, and respect, because if you don't take care of yourself first, then you can't give your all to the person that you love.

Many relationships can go back to being in a happy place if both people are willing to work on it together. Nobody is perfect in this world, and we all know this, yet many people forget this about their partner. Some people have not been taught the right way to behave towards others, and sometimes some guidance is all that's needed for them to express themselves in the right way.

The main thing that truly matters is if people make the best effort they possibly can to be the best partner they can be. And as a relationship coach, I have found that the people who do try their best, have the best relationships.

'When you're with the right person you'll understand why it didn't work out with anyone else...'

Sincerely,
Your Relationship Coach
Jacob Lucas

Printed in Great Britain
by Amazon

44114955R00076